James H. Cox
Confessions
A Freelancer's Guide
To The Church Market
of a
Moonlight
Writer

Confessions of a Moonlight Writer

©Copyright 1982. J M Publications,
A Division of J M Productions, Inc.
All Rights Reserved

No material in this book may be copied, reproduced, or used in any way without written permission from the author.

Library of Congress catalog card number: 80-70315
ISBN: 0-939298-00-7

JM Publications

A Division Of
JM PRODUCTIONS

P.O. BOX 837 • BRENTWOOD, TN 37027

To Sharon,
Robin, Jimmy, and Jodi Beth
who, perceiving my love affair
with a typewriter, indulge me
in it generously

Foreword

"Why is it," I wondered aloud, "that so many people attend writers' workshops and enrol in a journalism course, yet never get anything published?"

I was talking with a friend who, having started writing for publication just five years ago, has compiled an impressive record as a freelance writer in the church market. Her by-line has appeared in several religious periodicals and, currently, she's busy writing continuity material for religious radio.

"That's easy," she said. "There are a lot of people who are interested in writing, but only a few who want to write."

And, you know, she's right. Even a mild interest in journalism can propel one into workshops and writing courses. But a person must be driven by a more-than-average desire to sit down at a desk or typewriter and do the hard work of writing.

Confessions of a Moonlight Writer is a book for those who want to write, and those who want to write more successfully in the church market. If you belong to either category, you'll find invaluable advice here.

Having taught religious journalism for 15 years, I have never come across a more useful book for persons who want to break into the religious market. And even those of us who have been putting words on paper for quite a while can learn a thing or two from a man like Jim Cox.

Jim knows what he is talking about, and he talks about it in a clear, entertaining style. He's a real pro, with a great many years of writing and editorial work to his credit. But more importantly, he knows freelance writing from the other side of the editor's desk. He has received his share of rejection slips, as well as payment checks, from editors. What he brings to you in this book has been tested and refined in the school of experience.

This isn't a book for leisure reading, not the kind you can browse through once, then put on a shelf to collect dust. You'll use it as a working manual. At times you'll be inspired, as the author shares experiences out of his personal pilgrimage. But, more often, you'll be helped to deal with the hard-nosed realities of freelance writing.

There's no magic way to become a published writer. The dictionary will supply all the words you need. You will have to supply the creative energy needed to put the words together. But *Confessions of a Moonlight Writer* will supply invaluable guidance to help you channel those energies in the right direction.

Lucien Coleman
Southern Baptist Theological Seminary
Louisville, Kentucky

Preface

They looked at me in disbelief when I told them I was putting together a book for writers on how to break into the church market. I know they thought I was off my rocker for their facial expressions conveyed their surprise.

"Oh," said one, eyebrows raised. "A book about writing?"

"Yes," I assured, determined not to be daunted by anything. "It will help freelancers who want to write for religious publications know where to begin," I explained, trying to be convincing in my argument.

Again my friend nodded.

Again I had the feeling this non-writer had no earthly idea what a freelancer is, nor why one would need to know how to do his thing in the church market—whatever that is. He probably wondered why (and how) somebody would be trying to sell a church anyhow.

No matter. Folks thought Noah was a bit strange, too. At least, until it started raining.

You see, I have the distinct advantage of *knowing* these aspiring freelancers for the church market are out there, for I've met some of them. They predictably follow certain patterns. For example:

- They come out in droves to Christian writers' workshops, seminars, and conferences all over the country, clutching their little spiral-bound notebooks in which they jot down every 'tittle' that takes place. They hang on every phrase of every successful author on the program agenda. They never seem afraid to ask a profusion of questions, or to corner an editor for some personal evaluation of a piece they have just written.
- They are devoted readers of anything and everything that helps them pursue their insatiable desire to gain a byline in a church magazine. This will include devouring a wide line of religious publications regularly—from their own church, from others, and from the independent variety. They renew annual subscriptions to trade journals, such as *Writer's Digest* and *The Writer*, as each one lapses. They frequent book stores and libraries of all sorts, pouring over new volumes in search of fresh story ideas and grasping to discover untapped markets they never knew existed.
- They form and join writers' organizations on local, regional, and national levels where people of like faith share common goals. Together they find solace as they weep over rejection slips

and rejoice over a manuscript sale after a long dry spell. Some fraternal groups are even organized as writers' book clubs. Members receive regular mailings of new listings telling them how to become successful as part time or full time writers.

• Finally, the real proof these people exist, and do so in great numbers, is evidenced by the hundreds of thousands of unsolicited manuscripts editors of religious periodicals receive from them every year. These publications count heavily on this source of material, too, for many of their pages are filled by such copy. And while not every unsolicited manuscript is a real gem (indeed, most are rejected), an editor continues to welcome each and every one, hoping to discover among his authors a diamond in the rough. If he does, with little refinement and polish he may be able to take the writer's work and turn it into something that sparkles in the midst of his magazine. The editor may also sign his new-found discovery to produce a string of subsequent pieces in similar vein.

For all of these reasons, then, I know those who—and those who aspire to—freelance for religious publications, exist. The reader may have been previously successful as a writer in another market, but never have tried the religious side. Or, he may be in that great company I've encountered at writers' workshops and in the classroom who have never had anything published which they've written, but would give a right arm to see it happen.

For you, then, this book has been written. Perhaps it will answer some of the questions you didn't have an opportunity to ask before, or never knew whom to ask. If you're among those who have been promising yourself "one of these days I'm going to write," I hope it will inspire you to do something positive about that, regardless of your age, background, race, sex, education, experience, or circumstance. You'll never truly be satisfied until you try.

Another point worth making is, Christian writers are unique among the scribes. We have a decided edge over other free-lancers, I think, for we've got the greatest story ever told to share. Our job is to discover contemporary forms to communicate that message, still the same and as vital to a pagan world today as when Jesus walked the earth 2000 years ago.

The challenges, the opportunities, and the instruments to accomplish the task are all available to the creative writer who is serious about his pursuit. King David acknowledged, "My tongue is the pen of a ready writer" (Ps. 45:1). So it is with me. How about you?

Contents

May my words and my thoughts be acceptable to you, O Lord, my refuge and my redeemer!
(Ps. 19:14, TEV).

Certain scripture quotations used are taken from *Today's English Version:* Copyright © American Bible Society 1966, 1971, 1976.

1
If I Can, So Can Anybody!

A college sophomore's baptism into the world of freelancing

In 1978 *The Student*, a Christian collegiate magazine, shared with its readers the story of how this writer broke into freelancing for the church market. I'd like to recount it for you here. Perhaps it will help you understand "where I'm coming from" literally in my pilgrimage of becoming a published author.

Confessions of a Moonlight Writer*

You may find this difficult to believe at first, but I owe *The Student* a debt of gratitude for opening a "second" career for me.

It began nearly two decades ago when an article submitted to *The Baptist Student*, as the magazine was then named, was accepted for publication. As a result of that experience I began to realize the immense opportunities that exist for writers within the Southern Baptist Convention.

My first submission to a denominational magazine was called "A Summer at Ridgecrest." I never believed for a moment that it would be accepted. The feeling persisted within me that—as I was an "unknown" quantity, only a sophomore at the time—no Southern Baptist editor was going to publish one of my articles!

Imagine my ecstatic joy when I received a letter from David K. Alexander, then editor, informing me he would use my little contribution in the January 1960 issue. I'm sure neither of us dreamed then what this one article eventually would lead to. The passing of

---

*From *The Student*, May 1978. © Copyright 1978 The Sunday School Board of the Southern Baptist Convention. All rights reserved. Used by permission.

time would yield several hundred articles for Southern Baptist publications from the same typewriter that produced "A Summer at Ridgecrest."

In that original submission I described the opportunities that Ridgecrest Baptist Conference Center afforded those young people who were privileged to serve on its summer staff. As a veteran staffer of several years, I felt knowledgeable enough to put together a convincing advertisement for the rewards of a summer of service.

In having been successful in my first freelance attempt, I decided to try my hand at a second article. Can you guess who I sent it to? Alexander immediately replied that he would run my second entry in the January 1961 issue. It was called "So You're Thinking of Starting a BSU Newspaper." Here again, my subject was drawn from personal experience. At the time of writing, I was editor of the BSU paper on a large state university campus.

By that time I was encouraged enough to see if I could "cut the mustard" elsewhere or determine if my writing was limited strictly to the collegiate market. To my happy surprise I discovered *Church Administration* magazine, also published by The Sunday School Board, was eager to have articles from free-lance writers.

I often have wondered if it was my timing that did the trick in my early success with this magazine. *Church Administration* at that time had existed for only about three years. *The Student*, meanwhile, was observing its fortieth birthday. It seemed to me one of the big differences between them might be that *The Student* would have a larger, more developed backlog of regular writers because of its age. Therefore, I was not overwhelmed completely when "How to Prepare Biographical Sketches" was accepted for the January 1962 issue of *Church Administration*. I was well on my way toward establishing myself as that "known" free-lancer which I then believed I must become.

Two submissions—and two acceptances—followed that same year in *The Student*. In January 1962 the magazine published a second article on Ridgecrest, "Ridgecrest 'Mountaintop Experiences,' " which—you guessed it—also was drawn from personal encounter. (A note to anyone who wants to free lance: I have had better luck in getting manuscripts published when they dealt with subjects I knew something about from personal observation, knowledge, or experience than when they did not.)

My last submission to *The Baptist Student* was included in the October 1962 issue and was titled "Convention-Bound? I Dare

You!" In it I lauded the benefits of a campus BSU program had received by being well represented at an annual state Baptist student convention.

My college career behind me, I soon began to produce manuscripts frequently for several other denominational magazines. Although *The Student* had started my free-lancing avocation, I was ready to face other challenges as my interests and knowledge broadened. Before long my material was turning up in several other publications.

As time went on I became better acquainted with the editors, meeting and becoming close personal friends with some of them. Eventually I knew the kind of readership they had and the type of articles most of them were looking for. The one factor I could not know was if something I was submitting just had been done by another writer and had gotten to the editor first. This happened to me more than a few times.

There have been many interesting experiences in the years since *The Student* helped me become established as a moonlight writer. For a period of several years there was one magazine that I regularly had been published in which shied away from every article I sent, returning my manuscripts with accompanying lengthy explanations. I never figured what I was doing wrong, for the same editor had accepted earlier everything I sent. Then one day after I had been unpublished in this magazine more than seven years, to my astonishment the editor called with an idea for a story and asked if I'd like to do it. I quickly accepted the unexpected invitation and have been a semiregular in this periodical since.

I don't mind telling you that my toughest nut to crack became the greatest challenge of my writing career. I tried consistently and unsuccessfully for more than a decade to break into one of Southern Baptists' largest circulated monthlies. For years I analyzed what I was doing wrong. I studied the content of articles carried in the magazine, tried to develop approaches along those lines, edited, rewrote, shortened, lengthened, and met failure again and again.

Finally, after waiting a couple of years following a series of rejection slips, I jotted down three or four brief paragraphs about an emotional experience in sending our oldest child off to her first day of school. I titled it, "I Lost My Six-Year-Old Today!"

I sent it to the editor, and he bought it at once. (As I recall, it brought me the tidy little sum of $6.00; but I didn't mind that—I had set out to conquer and the victory was mine. Personal experience had won again!)

My avocation has provided opportunities to be a curriculum writer for *Ambassador Life* and *Leader, the Sunday School Builder*, stewardship lessons for children and teachers, *Bible Searchers, Bible Searchers: Teacher*, and *Children's Leadership*.

My largest single assignment has been the Vacation Bible School curriculum for older children (focus grades five and six) for the summer of 1972, a task which ran into more than four hundred hours of research, study, writing, editing, revision, and final typing. When I paid my income tax on that assignment, I discovered I would have come out ahead financially if I never had accepted the task! But the real reward came from the thorough Bible study required to complete the assignment.

Three books have come from my typewriter in these years of moonlight writing, although you never have read any of them because none has been published. The first never was submitted to a publisher. The second was rejected by publishers, as a book with a limited audience potential. The third, which I tentatively have titled "A Little Child Shall Lead Them," is currently making the rounds of publishers. It grows out of an appreciation for children and is directed to all who love, work with, and have small children themselves.

Several years ago I expanded my role as a free-lance writer to include other denominational publishers as well as our own. In addition, I accepted some copywriting assignments from advertising agencies.

Gone are the days of "A Summer at Ridgecrest." Now I am producing more "sophisticated" stuff like these more recent submissions: "A Quarter's Worth of Rinky Tink," an article about a coin-operated piano-playing museum in Underground Atlanta; "How Long Should the Preacher Preach?" (no explanation required!); "My Faithful Friend—My Outreach Leader"; "The Appaloosa: Horse of a Different Color"; and "Have You Seen What They've Been Doing with Flannelgraph?"

For whatever success there may have been in this venture, I acknowledge wholeheartedly the credit belongs to God, who distributed every talent. The scriptures tell us, "It is required in stewards, that a man be found faithful" (I Cor. 4:2). I am convinced God expects us to use the abilities we possess to their greatest potential.

Of course, I am not underestimating *The Student's* role in helping me become a free-lancer either. It's nice to hear a stranger say, "Now, where is it I've seen your name before?"

Thank you, *Student*, and perhaps you'll give someone else who needs an outlet for expression the same chance you gave me.

There's More Than One Way To Skin a Cat

At this juncture, I can't name anyone else who owes *The Student* the same debt of gratitude I do. Yet, I'm reasonably certain there are hundreds of others who could testify *The Student* gave them their initial exposure to the world of freelancing.

My own debut is surely no more dramatic than that of many others. (I just happened to get the idea of telling about it in order to sell another article!)

Some of my prolific freelancing friends didn't take a direct route into writing like I did but eased into it through a back door.

A teacher told me his auspicious beginning as a freelancer dates back to a time when an editor invited him to contribute a series of articles on a particular subject for his periodical. The teacher enjoyed his assignment so much he decided to launch a second career which has kept him steadily in front of a typewriter when he isn't in front of a classroom.

The wife of a former magazine editor confided in me she was "volunteered" by her husband who needed somebody to produce some articles on short notice. Her material is still turning up, I recently observed, now more than a decade after her "invitation."

A seminary professor provided the incentive and inspiration for yet another timid soul to shed her inhibitions and give freelancing a try. This lady, who is blind, is currently making a name for herself in the church market as her material shows up in more and more periodicals. All she needed was a little push from someone who believed in her to give her encouragement to step out on faith and try.

Several successful freelancers launched their careers as spin-offs from other activities. Some have been curriculum or lesson course writers, doing work for editors strictly by assignment, not venturing out with previously unsolicited material. Some have expertise as public speakers or conference leaders, but must acquire necessary disciplines to become good writers. Still others leave numerous diversions to join the ranks of moonlighting scribes. In fact, the ways people are lured into this "profession" are probably as many and as varied as the number of writers practicing this craft.

It really doesn't matter how one starts, of course. The point is, if he possesses the gift, he has an obligation to use it. To deny it is like burying one's single talent in the earth.

I was only a college sophomore when I submitted that first article for publication. Obviously, then, it doesn't take a genius to produce a manuscript that sells. (If I can, so can anybody!) Don't be afraid to try because you've never written before. And don't be afraid to try again because you've received a rejection slip, or two, or three, or four.

"Who you know" won't guarantee you a sale on most manuscripts, quite frankly, but there are ways you can greatly improve the odds by having a few "connections." We'll discuss these more in the next chapter.

Five Indispensables for Successful Freelancing

It seems to me, to be published frequently, a writer must acquire five basic qualities:

1. A God-given talent.
2. A marketable idea.
3. An ability to communicate that idea interestingly.
4. An audience (or market) for that idea.
5. An intuitive perception in good timing.

A story that lacks any one of the five already has a major strike against it. In this game, one strike and your story may be tossed out of the ball park completely.

Undergirding all five requirements is number one, the writer's own personal ability. In my opinion, one may read all the books, attend all the conferences, and gain all the degrees available in writing, but if he was born without the innate gift to write, he'll never be a very good writer.

Numbers two, three, and four relate to the article, idea, or story itself and are probably self-explanatory.

Number five refers almost entirely to chance—hoping that the story you've got is timely, that the editor has a need for it, that he has room for it, that he has nothing else on a subject similar to it which he'd prefer to run, and that you got it to him by his deadline. Of course, a writer can only second guess on most of these questions, but whether you sell an article or not may literally depend on whether you guessed correctly.

I don't know why you want to write, but I'd like to share some of my reasons for writing. Perhaps you'll identify with some of them, although you may never have put them all down in words before.

Why I Write

I don't remember when it began, or what the original inspiration was. I do remember Daddy bringing home an L. C. Smith Corona typewriter, already an antique when I first saw it.

I could have been no more than seven or eight years of age at the time, but that keyboard offered magnetic fascination to me. That may have been the catalyst that caused my initial attraction to words and their almost limitless combinations.

A few years passed, and I earned the reputation of neighborhood journalist, reporting everything of concern to the church and community through mimeographed "newspapers." I sold ads, composed editorials, covered news beats, handled interviews, and edited features supplied by a "staff" of adolescent proteges of similar persuasion.

Preoccupation with writing and "publishing" was so absorbing that for me communication through the printed word became preferable to the spoken one. While other students protested, I found solace and comfort in assigned themes, book reports, and term papers—almost anything requiring written communication.

Those little blanks on college entrance and job application forms and church talent surveys requesting interests and hobbies were always easy. Repetitiously I put down "writing." Anything after that was purely secondary and inconsequential.

To me, all one ever needed to transform himself into another place and another time was a notebook, a sharp pencil and an inquiring mind.

I'm grateful for that small measure of ability God dispensed to us scribes. It has brought this writer years of satisfying joy.

Sometimes I think of it as a trust from God to me. And with that trust comes inherent responsiblity, for the printed page has the power to transform men's souls. If there were no other reason but that one, I would write.

For all of this, I give thanks for this gift of life, this gift of time to share with those who literally read my thoughts.

A familiar verse in Ecclesiastes sums up my feeling for writing: "Whatsoever thy hand findeth to do, do it with thy might" (9:10).

Thank you, God, for sharing qualification number one with me, and for allowing me to have a fairly satisfactory batting average with numbers two, three, four, and five! Amen.

2
Take a Right Turn

Some tricks of the trade picked up along the way

Early in our oldest daughter's young life my wife and I discovered a rather pronounced interest in anything musical. She would clap her hands, hum, or even sing to the lilting melodies which poured forth on the radio, television, or phonograph. We knew we were fortunate to have a child so "musically inclined" for neither of us had been bitten by this same desire in our childhoods. We made up our minds, even if it took personal sacrifice, this child would not be denied lessons in piano if she desired them.

As it turned out, she welcomed that opportunity. While she has not become an accomplished pianist today, she plays relatively well. For her own—and our—pure enjoyment, she gives a concert almost daily in our home.

Our son, on the other hand, manifest an early interest in sports —sports of any kind and every kind. Several years ago we provided the opportunity for him to sign up for little league baseball and basketball. While he has not become an athletic star, every season it is obvious his ability to play has been tempered by being coached in the basics of these sports in previous seasons. His basketball team even won the championship one year, something that boy will remember for the rest of his life.

Why include these illustrations in a book about writing?

Because practice makes perfect. I haven't met any perfect writers yet, but I have met some that surely are way above the average. While all of them are born with certain natural attributes. I suspect repetition and plain old practice has had an awful lot to do with the degree of success they have achieved.

Every writer writes out of his own experience, his own background, talent, ability, knowledge, opportunity, environment, purpose, and interest. Writing is peculiar to an individual, and out of it successful writers develop their own style, their own modus operandi.

Much of one's ability to write is "caught" and not "taught." It is the result of an innate desire or natural ability placed in a person's very being by God himself. You either have it, or you don't. I believe there is very little latitude in between.

I could no more play the piano like my daughter than I could sprout wings and fly. I could have taken piano lessons—in fact, I had one or two when I was her age. But my parents quickly saw my heart wasn't in it! I didn't have anything against music, but it would have been wrong to have reprogrammed me from a love for writing into one as an entertainer. It just wasn't in my blood.

A post graduate student I know hopes to become an editor and a writer for his denomination. "It's all I *ever* wanted to do," he told me. But it has been a struggle for him.

His first year in a large state university was spent in agony studying medicine, pursuing the career his well-meaning mother and father had selected for him. He obliged them, but he was miserable.

After a year, he confided in his father to pursue it any longer would be a mistake. He had made one already which had cost his family $10,000. His father and mother relented; the youth's whole life brightened as the path cleared for him to pursue the career which had eluded him yet burned within his soul.

You just can't make a physician out of a scribe. It's pointless to try.

Where There's a Will ...

Is there help for the person with similar aspirations? It's plentiful. You just have to know what to look for.

For instance, there are a number of good texts available to assist the beginning freelancer. You needn't purchase every book on the subject for to do so would mean spending much of your time—and lots of your income—on learning how to write *without* writing. Plato, a well known Greek philosopher, theorized, "We learn by doing." That ought to be the writer's overarching objective, too.

For the sake of argument, however, let's say you've decided to invest in a few books to get you started. Which would be best?

If I were going to freelance for the church or denomination, I would begin with a volume by someone who's been successful in this avocation for years. *How I Write*, by Robert J. Hastings, published by Broadman Press, is such a comprehensive book and makes for delightful reading. It is specifically a manual for beginning writers.

I would look for some books which would help me say what I wanted to say well. The little volume, *How to Take the Fog Out of Writing*, by Robert Gunning, published by The Dartnell Corporation, will help you do just that. More will be said later on the subject of putting your best foot forward. Suffice it for now that this little volume, only sixty-four pages in length, will help you write clearly and concisely.

I used Hastings' and Gunning's books as texts for a basic course in religious journalism I taught at a seminary a few years ago. I believe they could be helpful to any aspiring freelancer.

We won't list other similar texts here, but refer the reader to the appendix at the back of this book. There you will find numerous supplementary texts for writers, particularly freelancers. One alternative to purchasing these books, of course, is to check with your local public library first. You may save yourself a good deal of cash in the process.

Another source for information on freelancing is two national monthly magazines, *The Writer* and *Writer's Digest*. Each carries stimulating, helpful articles for the professional as well as the novice writer.

Writer's Market, published by *Writer's Digest*, is an annual edition that suggests hundreds of sources for freelancers to get their work published. It also tells what editors are looking for, what they don't want, what they pay, and who to contact. I had to depend upon the generosity of a well-to-do relative to purchase this volume for me as a Christmas present a few seasons back. It *is* expensive, but I have seldom cherished a gift more.

There are also numerous conferences on writing held throughout the nation every year. Some are especially pitched toward freelancers, and several of these specifically toward the church and parish market.

Many denominations offer their own writers' workshops. Some are by invitation only, particularly when writing for curriculum or lesson course materials. An inquiry to the denomination's publishing headquarters for which you would like to write should provide answers to your questions about such opportunities.

Writer's Market includes a rather extensive, but incomplete, listing of writers' conference opportunities. A state-by-state breakdown shows you what's offered, who will benefit, and who to contact for information. The two magazines mentioned earlier also carry advertisements and listings for similar conferences.

If you are interested in attending any of these, you would do well to talk with someone who's been there before. Not often, but once in awhile you can go away from such an experience feeling disappointed, even cheated. Don't allow an overzealous attitude to get help prevent you from getting all you bargained for.

There are all types of writers' guilds, clubs, and organizations which—for a fee—will welcome your membership. Some are strictly for professionals, but others are for amateurs and semi-professionals as well. A rather extensive list appears in *Writers' Market.*

A word of caution is in order: Don't be taken in by unscrupulous charlatans in the writing industry who prey upon unsuspecting novices.

A prime example is illustrated in a little folder I picked up on a tract rack in a supermarket several years ago. It informed me, if I had ever thought about writing as a professional either full time or part time, I should enrol in their correspondence school for writers. The price tag was something like $400 for a few lessons, and they *guaranteed* I would be seeing my material in print within a short time. Hogwash! How many people have been taken in by such schemes?

It goes back to what we have already said. You have it, or you don't. Nothing can develop you into a good writer if it isn't first in your soul. Not $400. Not $4,000. Not any kind of *guarantee* your manuscripts will soon be in demand.

Unfortunately, sometimes magazines publish advertisements for writing schools or courses of this nature. While all are probably not deceptive, I know sad experiences of some would-be scribes who have been taken for a ride. My best advice is to pass up all such attractive sounding opportunities.

In some localities, night courses are offered by community colleges and state universities in writing. Adult education classes are provided elsewhere at reasonable rates. Check into these possibilities before going further from home.

A Systematic Approach

Now I'd like to share some personal rules for writing with you. These are tricks of the trade which have helped me turn out as many as a hundred or more freelance articles in spare time during a typical year. Most have been directed to the church market.

At the outset, let me state this is my writing "system" and mine alone. I do not have all the answers, nor would I suggest my plan precisely as stated will work for you. It works for me. I offer it with the hope at least some of these ideas will be helpful to those who have not yet firmly established their writing techniques.

I've shared this "system" with freelance writers in about two dozen conferences. Have you tried some of these ideas already?

1. Discover and write in the environment that is best for you.

Ideal circumstances may mean getting away from everything and everybody, or you may not require that at all. Time and place are important. You may be able to write fluently only at a certain time of day.

I once knew a writer whose sole opportunity to write was in the three-hour span each morning when her oldest child was at school and her preschooler was at kindergarten. Every day she cleared the breakfast dishes from her kitchen table. Placing her typewriter on the table in front of her chair, she put a stack of manuscript paper beside it and wrote prolifically.

A denominational editor friend of mine once said in print his best work was written between the hours of 10 p.m. and 2 a.m. You may scoff at that, but others tell similar tales. I've also run into writers who claim they can't produce anything except between 4 a.m. and 7 a.m. Either plan sounds impossible to me.

While I rise early, I'm generally not an early writer. I like to get the workday out of the way before getting serious about writing. My most productive hours have been late afternoons and evenings. This may be due to employment circumstances as much as anything else.

I mentioned environment. This is perhaps even more important than timing. Most successful writers do their best and most creative work when they are not unduly distracted. I can't begin to write in a room where television is turned on or other people are carrying on a conversation.

One of my most prized possessions is a small but adequate out-of-the-way room in our basement at home where I keep a desk, typewriter, reference books, and manuscript paper. Every writer needs his own private nook somewhere which he may truly call his own.

Our former home was situated on a deep lot with shade trees several hundred yards from the house. In the spring and summer months I could sit at a picnic table under those trees and produce more manuscript pages in an hour than I could inside the house in five. In a setting of picturesque scenery, warm gentle breezes, and birds singing, I was in an element totally conducive to writing. It was so much better than trying to compete with the many electronic marvels which distract a writer indoors!

Take stock of when and where you are trying to write. Is there a better time and place? Vary the place and the time you write. Seek to discover what's best for you.

2. Use your free time when you are not writing to think.

You can't write continually, even if your avocation is turning into full time work. Every writer needs time to reflect on his copy and to organize his thoughts for future articles.

Many people have laughed at me in writers' conferences when I told them my best time to think was shaving time in the mornings. Well, it is true, for some of the best ideas I ever had for an article or a whole series of articles came while I was standing in front of the mirror with a razor. Fortunately, I use an electric razor, so I haven't come close to hitting a jugular vein while being carried away with an idea!

A religious editor for whom I wrote for several years once allowed her best and most creative thinking time was while in transit. She used driving time to and from her office and to and from lunch to think. "I prefer to drive alone, and I keep the radio off," she declared. "It helps me organize my day in the mornings and reflect on what happened each day in the afternoons as I'm homeward bound."

Many professional writers learn early in the game to keep a pad or note card handy to jot down ideas which come at inopportune times. Just a word or a phase which surfaces in my mind is often the nucleus of an article. I write it down and put it aside to mull over and absorb, sometimes for days, weeks, or even months. Some of my best article ideas have developed in this way.

Years ago I started keeping a slip of paper by my bedside to jot the inevitable ideas on that would come during the night. For awhile, I had trouble the following morning reading what I had written. (I was thoughtful enough not to turn on the lamp, which would have awakened my sleeping wife.) After some practice, however, I learned to distinguish what I had written in total darkness.

Don't let your good ideas slip away from you. They may develop into some of your best work, either now or later. Think constantly, and put your ideas for stories into writing before it's too late.

3. *Know your intended audience.*

Study their backgrounds and analyze what they seem to be wanting to know. You can do it fairly easily by skimming through past issues of the periodical for which you intend to write. Attempt to learn the readers' general educational and training levels, their age range, whether they are largely church staff and denominational servants, laymen, or some other well defined group. Ask yourself: If I were in their shoes, would my subject appeal to me?

If you're writing for a youth publication, obviously you won't submit an article to the editor on "The Creative Uses of Building Blocks." By the same token, one called "The Layman's Role in Missions" probably would not fit a sacred music magazine. But one on "Church Staff Relationships" would go nicely in a publication for administrators of local parishes or churches. A series of devotionals, quite naturally, would fit a church meditation guide, but might not be appropriate for a magazine on religious architecture.

Do you get my drift? Become thoroughly acquainted with the interests and needs of those who will read what you have to offer. The best way to do it is to see what others are saying in those magazines.

4. *Be thoroughly acquainted with the style and requirements of the publication for which you intend to write.*

If it seems obvious in your study of a publication most articles begin with an illustration, it might be wise to use one. Are the articles often written in the first person, third person, or does it matter? Are most of them "how to" articles? Are they personality-oriented, or experience stories, or a general mix of a lot of forms? If you look carefully you may discover several preferences an editor has which will help you determine your approach. Then, go and do likewise.

Some editors will furnish mechanical specifications and tell you the types of material they are looking for, upon request. If you're unsure, it won't hurt to ask.

Analyze! Scrutinize! Harmonize!

5. *If possible, know your editor personally.*

Socrates, another great Greek philosopher, said, "Know thyself."

Cox, a lesser known freelance writer of contemporary vintage, said "Know thy editor."

Some time ago I was leading conferences in freelance writing across a deep South state. One day, I was surprised to find sitting in the group a man to whom I had previously mailed many manuscripts in years gone by. He had been the associate editor of a Christian family magazine published by one of the major evangelical denominations, but had recently resigned to enter the pastorate. I decided to capitalize on his presence by adding some spontaneity to the conversation.

"How many unsolicited manuscripts would you say you received in a year's time when you worked for the magazine?" I wondered aloud to my friend.

He thought for a moment. I dare say no one in the room was prepared for the answer he gave.

"I'd have to say, at least 10,000," he replied.

You could hear the gulps as people all over the room swallowed hard. I was sure many of them were thinking exactly the same thing: If my story has to compete with 9,999 others for space in that publication, how can I possibly succeed?

How? By contributing an article that is a cut above the average in writing technique, topic, treatment, timeliness, and taste. It must arrive on the editor's desk before any other article on a similar subject. It must be on a subject the editor knows his readers are interested in.

It seems to me there are yet other opportunities to distinguish your manuscripts from among the many an editor receives every day. One of the best ways I know is name recognition. If an editor, or one of his assistants, has "met" you—through a telephone call, a letter, a mutual friend, or better yet, in person—your manuscript is more apt to be read than if no one knows you at the receiving end.

Obviously, no editor could realistically read 10,000 manuscripts in full in a year. While most editors would never begin to receive that many, those who do need help in culling out desirable prospects. Knowing the editor, or more correctly, *having him know you*, could be your answer.

For sixteen years I had the good fortune of living in Nashville, Tennessee, a churchman's capitol if there ever was one. Seventh Day Adventists, Free Will Baptists, United Methodists, Presbyterians, the Churches of Christ, and Southern Baptists have (or have had) one or more of their agency headquarters here. The Methodist Publishing House in Nashville is the nation's largest religious printing concern. The Sunday School Board of the Southern Baptist Convention is the largest publisher of religious materials in the world. Other denominations headquartered here boast similar impressive records, although on a lesser scale.

With all this religious publishing activity, you may be sure it takes lots of editors to generate it. And the volume of editors is dwarfed by the number of writers required.

Early in my freelancing career I decided no harm could come from knowing as many editors on a first name basis as I possibly could. I sought them out, one by one, and looked for opportunities for social contacts with them in my own church, at my place of employment, over lunch, and by holding membership in organizations in which we had mutual interests. This has paid off in dividends I am enjoying now. My opportunities to "take an editor to lunch" were surely some of the best investments I ever made.

Most readers of this book won't have the good fortune of living in Nashville, Tennessee, or any other city which is able to call itself a religious headquarters mecca. What then?

Don't give up. Your chances to meet editors aren't nil.

How do you accomplish it?

Many religious printing houses send their editors out to speak and lead conferences in local parishes and churches, in college classrooms, at summer encampments and assemblies, and to numerous conventions and meetings where the people are. From time to time they even go out to cover a story themselves.

If you have the good fortune of being in the same city with an editor at the same time, by all means go to hear him and acquaint him with your interests. You might take along a manuscript for his publication, or tell him you'll be sending one along in a short time. Then, when you do mail him that manuscript, recall your meeting with him in a cover letter. If he likes your work, even if he may not be able to use the particular manuscript you've submitted, you may have triggered a response in his mind that will cause him to pull future submissions from you for thorough reading.

If you don't get to meet the editors you'd like to near home, perhaps you can plan a trip (vacation or business) to Nashville, New York, Chicago, Minneapolis, Washington, Grand Rapids, Philadelphia, or some other major religious publishing centers and call upon editors while there. Even a brief side trip out of your way might be worth it. But to be on safe ground, drop a note to the editors before you travel so you won't be disappointed should they be away from their offices when you arrive.

Mutual friends have also been sources for freelancers to market their material. I've known of several whose names were carried by editors' counterparts from conferences and summer assemblies back to the home office. Budding writers were called directly by editors and asked to submit articles. Don't hesitate to let your interests be known to anyone who is in a position to help you.

If this opportunity doesn't present itself to you, write an editor and tell him about yourself. Offer to take any assignment he feels you might be capable of handling. Share some of your background; where you have lived, your education and family status, what your talents and interests are, and the nature of your permanent employment. Share your own church affiliation and the roles you play in your local congregation.

If possible, pitch one or more article ideas his way. Don't be discouraged if he can't give you an immediate OK. He may need to see a manuscript in writing "on speculation" (which means, no commitment on his part) before he can accept it for publication.

Generally, a personal letter to make an editor's acquaintance is preferable to a telephone call. Editors often cannot be disturbed at a moment's notice. A letter may be read and answered at the editor's convenience, but a telephone call is at the caller's convenience.

Knowing the editor personally—even though you may never have met him face to face—will likely separate your material from the stack on his desk a lot quicker than if yours is only another name on a manuscript. What you know is important but so is who knows you.

6. *Understand any deadline you are given and make up your mind you are going to beat it.*

Start early. Experience often proves unexpected emergencies interrupt a writer and wreak havoc with even the best of schedules. A simple guideline might be, build in one extra week for yourself if you are doing a brief article at the editor's request. In other words, plan to complete it at least one week before it is due.

If you are writing curriculum (or lesson course materials), however, I would set my personal deadline no less than two months before the editor expects my copy, because *anything* can go wrong. And if you think it's not a sin to be late with an editor, you'll quickly learn that many regard that one as cardinal.

Some time ago I received a phone call from a panicky editor. He had just learned alterations were requested in a segment of the Vacation Bible School material for which he was responsible. His superiors asked that it be rewritten after a team of writers had submitted it shortly before press time. In desperation, he begged, "Is there any way you could write it for me?" I assured him I could supply the seventy-four typewritten pages he desired by his deadline of eight weeks. He made a flying trip to my home the next week to give me all the particulars on what he wanted.

When he left town and the dust settled, I started writing. For the next two weeks I wrote constantly in my spare time. In less than three weeks the completed manuscript was on his desk.

I'll never forget the letter which arrived a short time later from him. "How did you do it?" he asked. "You must have enlisted your wife, your children, your secretary, and all the children you teach at church to help you get it done so fast," he exclaimed. It was not a put-down on the quality, I don't think, but rather surprise over beating the deadline so handily.

I really had rather not take an assignment than submit it late. I've seen writers who couldn't get it all together literally cut out of writing jobs forever by their editors. It's a black mark against a freelancer's name which seasoned writers know they can and must live without.

7. *Know your subject.*

If you are not personally acquainted with the theme about which you are writing, be able to research it thoroughly.

An editor once asked me to submit four articles on homes of differing cultures. He told me I could select the four types of dwellings I wished to write about. I chose the Eskimo's igloo, the Indian's tepee, the Japanese pagoda, and the Hong Kong boat people's home, the junk. Frankly, I didn't know a thing about any one of them except what they looked like in picture books. My own set of encyclopedias contained some information but not enough to help me flesh out the stories. Where was some information?

The natural place to look was the public library. Unfortunately, the branch just two blocks from my house was fresh out of books on igloos, tepees, pagodas, and junks. My attention turned to the main public library downtown, seventeen miles away. It was worth the trip. I returned with a stack of stories about other cultures which provided more information than I could ever hope to use in four articles.

I trust you don't make the mistake I did on that particular assignment, however. Why I did it I'll never know, for I certainly *knew* better. I developed the rough drafts, edited, polished, retyped, and mailed them off to the editor. An acknowledgement that they had arrived soon came.

I forgot about them and went about other writing pursuits. A few weeks later, I received a letter from the editor's manuscript assistant concerning those four articles on igloos, tepees, pagodas, and junks.

"Where'd you get your information?" she pondered.

I froze. Not in years had I forgotten to include what she had just asked. But I had this time. The worst part of it was, I had adapted ideas from so many different sources. Nowhere had I written down the name of even one of those books. Talk about eating crow. The letter I wrote her was purely one of humiliation! I vowed right then and there to check *everything* I did from then on to be sure any reference the manuscript assistant needed would already be supplied, typed neatly in the right hand margin beside the information it referred to.

(Just before writing this particular chapter, I completed a sixteen-page manuscript for a religious editor and shipped it off. I have just now gone back and checked my carbon of that article. There are no less than forty-nine references documented in the right hand margin of that manuscript. I think I've learned my lesson!)

Another important point to knowing your subject is to be willing to admit your idea fizzled if you get into it and find it has.

About a decade has elapsed since an editor of a denomination other than my own asked me to prepare an article for him on the occult. To begin with, I had to look up the meaning of the term, since that one wasn't in widespread use in those days. Webster, I found out, suggested it pertained to "alchemy, magic, astrology and other arts and practices involving use of divination, incantation, magical formulae, etc." I found Webster's next definition of occult most appropriate: "beyond the scope of understanding; mysterious."

I don't believe I ever found any subject further beyond my grasp than this one. I poured through book after book trying to get hold on the subject, yet it remained elusive. I think even now, after several years' exposure to it, I don't really have any basic understanding of it.

Finally, I had to throw up my hands and admit to my editor friend I blew it. I hope he asked somebody else to write it; I never had the courage to bring it up again.

You needn't try to trick an editor into believing you know something concerning a subject about which you know absolutely nothing. He won't be fooled, and he won't try to fool his readers with unfounded (or confounded?) trivia. Shakespeare would call it "much ado about nothing." Be honest enough to tell your editor you've bitten off more than you can chew after exhausting all the possibilities at your disposal. Most editors will understand and will appreciate your candor and sincerity.

One final thing. Personal experiences have always been easiest for me to write about. (You say you've found that out already?) I can draw upon things that have happened to my friends, in situations I have observed, to my own family, or to me, and illustrate a story much better than I can produce one based on heavy research. The words flow so much more easily when I'm intimately acquainted with the subject.

I would not venture to say *every* freelancer will profit by this rule, for some may prefer other techniques. When you discover the type article which suits your style best—personal experience, how to, fiction, research, or whatever—capitalize on it. You'll likely produce more and better ideas and completed copy in a shorter period of time than if you don't.

8. *Accept rejection slips graciously.*

What is a rejection slip, anyway? It's often a rather impersonal form letter or card stating that while an editor greatly appreciates your taking the time to send him a manuscript, he is returning it "herewith." There is frequently something to the effect your work does not meet "our publishing objectives at this time," or some similar phrase.

I'm going to withhold my pride and quote verbatim from a typical rejection slip (of which there are many) in my collection:

> Thank you for sending the enclosed material to (name of publication). We regret that we are unable to use it at this time. We are sorry that our large amount of correspondence makes it impossible for us to answer all submissions personally. Please be assured that we appreciate your interest. Thank you again for considering us.
>
> Sincerely,
>
> The Editors

It arrived on a white sheet about the size of a postal card and was printed in green ink. There was no handwritten acknowledgement anywhere on the card. My labor of love (a manuscript I had peddled to several denominational publishing houses previously), though dog-eared and worn by now, was neatly gem-clipped to the rejection slip.

What went wrong? One editor was kind enough to gently point out some mistakes, at least, as he witnessed them, and to encourage me in my work. My advice to any would-be freelancer would be, listen to any editor who goes to the trouble of telling you how you may strengthen a manuscript. There is really nothing to be gained, and potentially much to be lost, in getting mad at an editor and in harboring a grudge. The best thing you can do is to forget it and proceed with your next writing endeavor.

Early in my writing career, I came dangerously close to crossing myself up permanently with a particular editor who presided over a rather influential monthly religious magazine. I desperately wanted the exposure in her publication, and I was successful in several successive attempts at getting my material placed in it. Then, I made a costly mistake.

In a youthful and inexperienced attempt to take on what I saw as a major faux pas in the life of a denominational agency (or "the establishment," as we might call it now), I saw my dreams crumble. The skilled and very wise editor took the time to decimate my manuscript sentence by sentence, and to write me a very long letter. She went into great detail about why it was an inappropriate subject, even if it was rewritten.

To my credit, I did not fire off any reaction to her. But to my discredit, I said to myself, "I'll show her." I decided to penalize her by withholding future articles—at least, for the time being—from her publication. Oh, what a tangled web we weave, when first we practice to deceive! As it turned out, *I* was the one who was deceived, of course, but I was too much a novice to realize it then.

I continued to come up with story ideas which would be perfect for her magazine. But my pride had been wounded, and for a time I wouldn't bend to the pressures mounting within.

Finally, I could stand it no longer. I fired off manuscripts to this editor with the same rapidity I had exercised earlier. But something had happened in those intervening months. My editor developed a backlog of other writers, and every manuscript I sent was returned with a rejection slip attached.

For three or four years I believed I had cut my own throat and would reap my just rewards forever. When I had resigned myself completely to that fate, out of the clear blue a call came one day from this same editor suggesting a rather extensive article on a subject she knew I knew something about.

After I picked myself up off the floor, I told her of course I would be delighted to supply it. I went to work right then, and the manuscript which resulted was probably one of the better articles I have done. From that day forward, I never had another problem getting into that editor's magazine again.

Did she realize the game I was playing, and was she fighting fire with fire? I've often wondered about that and never asked. I've learned to let bygones be bygones. But the most important lesson I learned was to accept rejection of my work graciously. It's a no-win situation for everybody concerned when you don't.

9. *When a manuscript is rejected, salvage it if you can.*

If the editor is interested in your idea but requests a rewrite, incorporate his ideas in your revision and submit it again. If he just isn't interested, and your manuscript can fit another publication, send it.

I'm going to bare my soul once again and tell you some more secrets which may shock you. If they don't shock *you*, they may cause some of my *editors* to have cardiac arrests!

I've had the good fortune to write for some years for an editor who buys every article I send. (See, I told you they would be shocking!) I can't account for that, but in one twenty-month period this same editor accepted twenty manuscripts from me. Some of these were originally prepared for other editors, who rejected them. With little or no changes in wording I have been able to redirect these manuscripts to this particular editor and meet with success every single time. If I can do it, others certainly can and do.

If you try two or three or four editors with a particular article and are turned down by each one, don't discard your unsold manuscript yet. Sooner or later, editors are promoted, transferred, retired, in rare cases fired, or die. Time could be in your favor.

I once pulled out oodles of manuscripts which had all been turned down several years earlier. They had been collecting dust on a closet shelf while I bided my time. Eventually, there was a change in editorships on each of the magazines to which these articles were originally submitted. I mailed them out again, updating only as necessary, and in some cases changing nothing. All of them sold their first time out.

Once or twice I have even sold a manuscript to an editor who years before had rejected it, *without changing one word*! My explanation for that is, (a) their "publishing objectives" changed, or (b) they had short memories. Either way, patience paid off.

Don't limit your manuscripts to *one* denomination, either. Nearly every evangelical group publishes its own Christian family magazine, its own devotional guide, and other similar pieces of literature. Sometimes with minor changes in terminology, what has been rejected by a Presbyterian editor may do very nicely in a Methodist publication, and vice versa. Consider all of the avenues open to you when a manuscript is turned down. Never throw it away. Somewhere out there an editor may be waiting for just what you have to say.

10. Don't ever send a manuscript to more than one editor at the same time.

It could be the kiss of death. Let me illustrate.

Suppose you have decided to speed up your chances for getting a manuscript into print by sending it at the same time to two editors who work for the same publishing firm. Your identical articles reach the desks of two editors in different parts of the building in the same morning's mail. Both editors go to coffee break that day at the same time, bump into one another, share a table, and begin to relay what they are finding in the mail these days. If your name is mentioned, it will soon be changed to "mud." In fact, you'll probably be out of future writing pursuits for these editors for awhile, perhaps even permanently, and they may share what you have done with other editors. The potential damage to your freelancing career simply isn't worth the gamble.

Even if you send the same article at the same time to two editors who work for *different* publishing outfits, you're just as dead should *both* of them accept your manuscript for publication. In fact, you're playing an even more dangerous game than simply ruining your reputation as a freelancer. If by any conceivable margin of error your article finds its way into print in *two* publications, you could be threatened with a lawsuit by one or both parties.

You can avoid such risks by contacting only one editor at a time. If the first one you send your work to says "no thanks," you have every legal and honorable right to pursue it with a second editor, or as many as it takes to sell it, *one at a time*. Don't jeopardize your reputation by being overanxious or impatient. You could bite off more than you can chew if you do.

11. Obey copyright laws!

In publishing, you must give credit where it is due. You can borrow words in conversation which you simply can't help yourself to without legal complications when you put them in print. Quoted material of any kind from any published source should be documented. Often, it will require written permission from the publisher, not the author, before you may use it.

Generally, it is up to the writer of church publications to secure written permission from the copyright owner when including copyrighted material in manuscripts. A copy of that permission should be furnished with the manuscript when it is submitted to the editor. It is also wise to have a second copy (photostat or carbon) of the permission to clip to your own carbon of your manuscript for safe-keeping should any questions arise later.

Permission to use copyrighted material is usually easy to secure, if you agree to provide proper acknowledgement in the manuscript. Most publishers will state precisely how the permission must appear. A typical acknowledgement may read like this one I was recently granted by a publisher:

> Arthur B. Rutledge, *Mission to America* (Nashville: Broadman Press) p. 24. All rights reserved. Used by permission.

Only once have I ever had to pay a fee to use quoted material. Ironically, that manuscript never sold, either.

Obtaining copyright permission is just part of the writing task.

It's like washing the dishes at our house. The one who does it knows he's not finished until the pots and pans, which don't fit into the automatic dishwasher, are scrubbed by hand, the counter is cleaned, and the food is put away. It would be easier to load the dishwasher and walk out, but somebody still has to handle the other duties. Editors, for the most part, aren't all that eager (nor do they have time) to do for you what you can do for yourself. Become professional! Furnish copyright permissions *with* your submissions.

12. *Prepare your copy the way you would expect to receive it if you were the editor.*

Or, do unto others.

In the style manual I created for my own editorial staff this statement appears: *How you look is so loud I can't hear what you say.*

The appearance of your copy either pegs you as an amateur or an experienced and accomplished writer. First impressions are important ones in writing. How you present yourself through the appearance of your submission to an editor may tell him a great deal about what he will find within its pages, even before he reads it. Smudges on the outside may suggest sloppiness on the inside; disregard for form may indicate lack of attention to detail.

I feel so strongly about this, a little later I am devoting a chapter to the subject of how to sell yourself, and your manuscripts, based on looks. The form in which you submit your copy is an integral and very important part of becoming successful in writing. Don't sell it short.

13. *Keep your dictionary handy and don't be afraid to use it.*

Nothing tells an editor you aren't too sure of your English any sooner than misspelled words, or those you use incorrectly. It doesn't take much longer to look up a word to be sure about it, and it could mean the difference in qualifying your manuscript for a full reading or partial one. When an editor runs across a lot of misused or misspelled words, his initial inclination may be to toss that manuscript aside.

Incidentally, while on the subject of references, another good help is a thesaurus, a cross reference of thousands of words with similar meanings. A good one I can recommend is *Roget's International Thesaurus*. I use it often.

If economics is a problem, there are many inexpensive thesauruses available, some in paperback form. A good one will pay you dividends if you are thinking seriously of freelancing in the years to come. It's a small price to pay for the benefits you will derive.

14. *Approach your writing with a flair for freshness, crispness of words, and, above all, clarity and brevity.*

This is another subject to which a whole chapter will be devoted a little later. As an editor, I feel very very strongly about this subject.

Why provide a lot of needless jargon an editor can't use? Pure rhetoric pacify the scribe!

Use words which convey meaning, and nothing else. These lend sparkle to lifeless pages, and clarity to sentences which are out of focus. Choose your words deliberately, and don't throw anything into the soup mix you don't need. My college freshman English teacher frequently reminded his students: "It ain't what you say, but the way that you say it!" The grammar was atrocious, but the message spoke volumes. Dressing a manuscript for public consumption means choosing just the right words — and no more.

15. *Make your lead strong enough to propel the editor and your prospective reader into your article.*

A lead, as any serious student of journalism knows, is the first two or three paragraphs (often referred to as "graphs" of a story). It's what, hopefully, moves the reader from glancing at an article to getting seriously into it — enough to stay with it to the end.

An old cigarette commercial used to admonish, "It's what's up front that counts." Well, freelancers, it still is.

If the reader is turned off by your initial approach, he may never reach your conclusion. The lead is the vehicle which propels him into your story.

Instead of trite, factual, or uninteresting leads, try some of these approaches, experimenting with several in developing your writing style:

- Use startling statistics (as the *Reader's Digest* often does).
- Begin with humor, preferably relating it to your overall theme or purpose.

- Answer a question by briefly giving a success story; then go into what led up to it.
- Use the interview dialog, citing key points in your article.
- Incorporate human interest, almost always a sure fire attention getter.
- Share a personal experience, or one that happened to someone you know.
- Quote an applicable scripture.
- Offer a personal theory — and set out to prove it.
- Give a measure of something successful, such as an event.
- Give brief quotes from several people which pertain to the subject at hand.

Of course, the type of writing you are doing will dictate which method you will use. You would not, for example, ordinarily begin a devotional by offering a personal theory and setting out to prove it, although even that lead is a possibility. You would be more likely to tell how much — or by what percentage — a local congregation over-subscribed its annual budget before telling how they did it.

Which of the suggested leads would you be following? This time you've given a measure of something successful, such as an event (in this case, pledging the budget). After you've gotten the reader's attention, you give him the step-by-step approach this particular congregation took to accomplish it.

You'll want to experiment with several of these possibilities, and develop some of your own. The goal is to get the reader well into your story so he won't want to put it down before he's finished reading.

Perhaps a word should also be said about heads for articles. As an editor, I'm a stickler for creating as many imaginative, catchy, and clever headlines as possible for our publication every week. Sometimes I literally spend an hour or more developing a head for a certain article. I'm sure that's more time than is required, but I believe heads should flag an audience's attention, instead of waving them on.

One of the best heads I ever read appeared over a weather report in a daily newspaper several years ago. It summed up the story in this one line: "How greyed thou art."

If you have a good suggestion for a title for your manuscript, include it on the copy paper. It will be the prerogative of the editor to decide whether to accept or reject it. But your suggestion may be much more imaginative than his, and he will be grateful to have it.

16. Don't try to cover too much in your story.

The reader's attention span is not infinite, and your story may become tiresome and confusing for him if you get too detailed or try to expand it beyond its original premise. Keep in mind the fact a story doesn't have to be *eternal* to be *immortal.*

The first time an editor purchased one of my manuscripts, then reduced it to little more than half its original content, I was cut to the quick. I thought it was cruel and inhuman treatment, although I dared not tell him so. Months later, when I had recovered some of my loss of dignity, as I read that article then appearing in print, I realized the editor had a point. What he had done was to trim away the fat, the extraneous details which contributed nothing to my story. I had woven in a lot of extra stuff that would only bog the reader down.

I'm thankful I had the opportunity to learn this lesson early in my writing career. It prepared me for numerous similar experiences later. It's one of those lessons writers acquire in the school of hard knocks, although it can often be a rather painful one.

17. When you must stop writing before an article or an assignment is completed, keep an idea hanging.

Keep something going instead of quitting when you reach a natural break. It's so much easier to get back to. Let me illustrate.

Plenty of times I have been right in the middle of composing a story at the typewriter when I would be called to the supper table, or to see a favorite TV show, or go to some prearranged appointment. Rather than typing on a few more seconds to the end of the next graph, or section, chapter, illustration, or whatever the next natural break was, I'd just stop. Right in the middle of a sentence — not even waiting to arrive at a period.

This little rule has helped me get back into my work more easily than anything else I've tried. It has spared countless hours of lost time rereading previous pages to reorganize my thinking and decide where to begin next. It just makes sense that, if you're in the middle of a sentence, there's only one starting point. You pick up where you left off.

Several years ago in a religious writing conference an editor shared with the group this very same philosophy. For years, she confided, she left paper in the typewriter when interruptions came in her writing. She always went back to it much more readily than she would have if she had paused at a natural stopping place. I didn't say anything, but smiled. Great minds run in like channels, I thought.

18. Do take breaks away from your writing.

Good ideas simply won't come consistently. And even when they do come, you can jot them down for future reference (as I frequently do), and enjoy some other diversion for awhile. All work and no play, you know.

I classify myself as a "spurt" writer. I write tenaciously, laboriously, and faithfully for a period of a few weeks, using almost all the discretionary time available to me for writing. Then, all of a sudden, I complete the last article on my current list, my assignments are all mailed off to my editors, and I'm a bird out of a cage! I say to my wife, "Come on, honey. Let's go out and celebrate." We take off to some fancy restaurant we've been wanting to try.

For the next few weeks, I pursue some diversion from writing, although I'm jotting down ideas for future articles all the time. I may paint the exterior of the house, or plant a garden, take a vacation, plan and conduct writing or Bible teaching conferences, or make several business trips. I recently took three months off from freelancing to convert the basement of our home from storage to living space.

I've sat through many a writing conference and heard some very famous writers who would not agree with me on this approach at all. Most of them have encouraged, "Write something every day." If that works for them, and for you, fine. I don't have the time or the inclination to do it, and I love to write almost as much as I love to eat. Diversion to other activities is stimulating and invigorating for me.

One can't afford to ignore his family, his church, social contacts, and other meaningful relationships and activities which greatly enhance the quality of his life. He needs time to commune with God, with nature, and with those around him. Time off for good behavior makes sense to me.

By the same token, a writer should never forget this special talent God has given him. He should use it frequently, and to the best of his ability.

These, then, are the rules I have adopted in writing. I hope they will be helpful to you, and will stimulate you to serious thinking about how you may develop your own "system" which enhances what you say and how you say it.

What's bugging you?

There are yet a few questions that come to my mind which you might like to have settled. Again, these are my own opinions, and you are not bound to follow them. You must do what *you* are comfortable doing.

Q. Just how important are outlines? Do you work from them?

A. All my life, I've been told they are extremely important. Most of my colleagues outline every article they turn out. However, I never put an outline on paper. For this very book, I'm working from a list of chapter titles only. I am developing the material as we go along, and drawing upon that which I have used in writing conferences.

This may be foreign to what your English teacher has told you. All I can say is, it works for me.

I do generally organize an outline in my head before beginning a story, but never on paper. It's an obstacle that tends to limit the creative thought processes as I go along. If you feel you need the security of a written outline, however, I would not hesitate for a moment to develop one.

Q. Did you say you compose at the typewriter?

A. Very definitely. It requires less effort, is quicker, and is much easier to read. The only time I ever write in longhand is if I'm too far away from a typewriter, such as when I'm away on a trip, or out in a nature setting.

My style is to compose in the typewriter, polish by hand, then — usually — retype the finished copy *once*. If I'm not satisfied with the polishing, I will retype twice or even three times. On a long assignment, such as curriculum, the final typing alone may run into thirty, forty, fifty, or even a hundred hours or more and nearly drive you bananas if you're typing it yourself.

Incidentally, I have assumed all along anybody desiring to freelance has had Basic Typing 101. If not, don't go another day without making plans to enrol in an adult education typing class somewhere. The hunt-and-peck method will drain you physically and emotionally as it quadruples your typing time, even if you've perfected the system. And if you're thinking about paying a typist to turn out your finished manuscripts, forget it. Good ones now charge a dollar or two per finished page! You'll lose a bundle on every assignment if you go about it that way.

A professional typing course will be one of the best investments you ever made if you can't handle a keyboard quickly. You will be grateful forever you took it.

Q. How many notes do you take from which you develop a story?

A. I was surprised some time ago to read an article by one of my peers, a professional whom I respect in this business very much. He was offering suggestions on how to write feature articles. He said a reporter or writer should take as much as three to six times the notes he will actually use in a finished article. Preposterous, I thought. I don't believe I've ever thrown away three to six times the material I had in doing *any* story. My editors may have thrown it out later, but I seldom take even twice the notes I intend to use in an article.

Sometimes in an interview situation I write down things a subject says to me which I have absolutely no intention of including in my article. I do it because it would be too uncomfortable not to. For my own benefit, I draw brackets around those particular notes. When I am going over them later, I cross out that section.

Each writer will have to be his own judge about how many notes to take. It's easier for me to have less to wade through when it comes time to write, but if you need the support of mountains of notes, by all means take them. I suspect in time you will begin to make fewer and fewer notes as you gain more and more confidence in your ability.

Looking Back

Summarizing what we have said, let me suggest you attempt to develop a writing "system" (including time; environment; information about periodical audiences, subjects, and editors; copy preparation; and style) which is uniquely your own. It must evolve through trial and error, and may only be acquired through lots of practice.

One of the biggest dividends that will come to you when you have fully developed your personal system will be a renewed enthusiasm for this gift of God we know as writing.

At a summer religious writers' conference in 1969, juvenile author Lee Wyndham gave me a copy of her own "Ten Commandments for Writers." I've kept them close to where I write ever since. I'd like to pass them along to you:

1. Love thy subject.
2. Love thy reader.
3. Thou shalt not begin without prior meditation.
4. Thou shalt know thy characters as well as thou knowest thyself — even better!

5. Thou shalt not begin until thou knowest whither thou goest, and have a well-thought-out plan for the journey.
6. Thou shalt stop when they story is finished.
7. Thou shalt not worship thy words as images graven in precious marble.
8. Thou shalt make a clear, dark-ribbon copy of thy work.
9. Thou shalt study thy markets diligently, and only then send thy manuscript into the world.
10. Thou shalt not brood upon its fate, but set about the workings of thy next project, with good will and a high heart.*

Try it. I believe you'll like it.

---

* *Writing for Children and Teenagers.* © Writer's Digest Books, Cincinnati, 1980. Revised Edition. Used by permission.

3
My Five Infamous Friends

And other linguistic atrocities which crop up now and then

Someone has said, "If all the grammarians in the world were placed end to end, it would probably be a good thing."

My guess is, the person who said it didn't make straight A's in English composition either, and carried a grudge.

I once had an English teacher who frequently remarked, "A preposition is a bad thing to end a sentence with." I don't know who she was fooling — perhaps it was not me she was speaking *to*. (Catch that?)

An editor and writer, one of my protégés, sent me this clipping from some source, under the title of "Good Riting":

> Each pronoun agrees with their antecedent.
> Verbs has to agree with their subjects.
> Don't use no double negatives.
> A writer mustn't shift your point of view.
> When dangling, don't use participles.
> Join clauses good, like a conjunction should.
> Don't use run-on sentences you got to punctuate.
> About sentence fragments.
> It's important to use apostrophe's right.
> Don't abbrev.
> Check to see if you any words out.
> In my opinion I think that an author when he is writing shouldn't get into the habit of making use of too many unnecessary words that he really does not need.
> Last but not least: Lay off cliches.

I'll bet you smiled inside as you read at least some of those. They remind me of that old cliche: *Don't do as I do; do as I say do.*

You think writers don't make basic grammatical blunders? Look at this sentence copied verbatim from a religious newspaper published recently:

> People who need information about the way the Cooperative Program money is spent is asked to contact our missionary for an appointment.

The noun (people) and the verb (is) obviously do not agree. Many elementary school children know that. But neither the man (a college and seminary graduate) who dictated the copy or (should we use a double negative and say "nor"?) his secretary who typed it caught the disagreement. Writers for religious magazines and newspapers certainly have no corner on perfect English, do they?

Mark Twain once said, "The difference between the right word and the almost right word is the difference between lightning and the lightning rod."

The degree of success enjoyed by freelancers rises and falls with the copy they produce. If they don't have a basic working knowledge of their own language, the editor who catches their inevitable grammatical indiscretions may suffer migraines. And the poor writer may suffer the fate of having his work returned because he didn't follow grade school lessons about antecedents, tenses, and punctuation.

If this is your problem, consider enroling in an adult education basic grammar class. It need not wound your dignity; everybody in that class will be there for the same reason. Like the alcoholic, they are big enough to admit they need professional help. You will never develop your potential as a writer if you can't command the King's English. Survey the advantages of such a course if you need it. There's just no room for 'sloppy copy' on most editors' desks.

Your choice of words, and the appearance of your manuscripts (to be discussed in a later chapter) will weigh mightily on the editor who receives them. You'll want to do all you can to make that first impression as favorable as it can be.

Robert Gunning's little book, *How to Take the Fog Out of Writing*, mentioned earlier, will be an invaluable aid to any writer seriously interested in decreasing extraneous jargon in his copy. I commend his Fog Index formula highly, and suggest you experiment with it on some of your own copy.

Bob Hastings (*How I Write*) suggests the average American reads on a sixth grade level. Does that surprise you? Meanwhile, many of us forget all that and continue to write for people who should have completed graduate school in order to fully comprehend us.

Eons ago, in journalism school, we were taught never to include more than thirty words in any one sentence. That rule has stuck with me and indicted me thousands of times. It's still a good one to follow. Today, when I feel my sentences becoming wordy, I stop to count. Shorter sentences just naturally bring one's material a whole lot closer to that desirable reading level of sixth grade, too!

I hope you'll pardon me for dipping into my own background again. There is a reason for it which you will soon see.

My professional career in religious journalism was launched in 1959. It is an almost unnerving thought for me to realize millions and millions of words have passed through my hands in these ensuing years. Hundreds of thousands of them were written by me; millions more were contributed by other scribes.

For nine years, I held various public relations positions within my denomination. The volume of press releases I personally wrote sometimes exceeded one thousand annually.

For another seven years, I was responsible for proofreading and editing the daily copy of five advertising copywriters. At the same time, I was editing a monthly employe magazine for a religious publishing house.

In addition, I've edited a bimonthly alumni publication for five years, and a quarterly national continuing education newsletter two years.

Since 1975, I've been on the receiving end of countless thousands of institutional news releases like those I used to produce. My present responsibility requires me to scrutinize other people's copy every day. The average is between twenty and fifty news items in a typical day's mail.

On the sidelines, all this time I've been moonlighting for religious publishers almost incessantly. My typewriter has produced reams of curriculum materials, devotionals, advertising copy, articles, and news stories for several denominations. I could not begin to imagine how many words all that adds up to, but surely in the millions, and perhaps billions.

Have I learned anything from all this exposure to our language?

Yes, a great deal.

First, my eye looks much more critically for grammatical and typographical errors than it did before. This experience has helped me rather quickly discern if a writer seems to be communicating or not.

Some writers raise questions — but never answer them; some require supporting data — but omit it; some use proper terminology — but write above their readers' level of understanding; some state a proposition — but offer insufficient background information to prepare their readers for it.

Friends v. Foes

In my present responsibility, when I began reading millions of words annually produced by various editors and writers, I was shocked. It was immediately obvious certain words and phrases were needlessly repeated in the bulk of the copy coming across my desk. As I put together a manual of style (a book of 'laws' for consistency's sake) for the editorial staff of our publication, I could not help acknowledging some of the greatest offenders.

I have labeled these "my five infamous friends." Frankly, at times a prerequisite for gaining a journalism career position in my own denomination seems to hinge on one's determination to sprinkle these five offensive terms liberally throughout his copy.

What are these five tired, overworked, and extraneous words and phrases?

that
new
special
designed to
served as

Let me illustrate.

"I feel *that* so often we think *that* we know all *that* there is to know." Better: "I feel so often we think we know all there is to know." Deleting this one repetitious word all of us are guilty of overusing shortens and improves copy many times. The word *that* simply isn't necessary to the meaning of this sentence, now is it?

"This is a *new* idea which will transform your planning." Better: "This is an idea which will transform your planning." Advertising and TV have conditioned us against being stopped cold over anything being *new* any more. *New* is understood by the reader. Presumably, you wouldn't be espousing an idea's revolutionary characteristics if they weren't a bit unique in the first place.

"There will be a *special* session for adult leaders in the auditorium." Better: "Adult leaders will meet in the auditorium." Here's another example of a word whose welcome advertising and TV have worn out. Nothing under the sun is *special* any more now that everything is! What makes a session for adult leaders, or item, or person, or thing any more *special* than another? Obviously, only in the eye of the beholder (writer, promoter, planner, etc.).

"This kit is *designed to* help teachers in their quest for Bible teaching helps. "Better: "This kit will help teachers in their quest for Bible teaching helps." I don't know how it is with you, but when I think of a designer, I picture someone who draws dresses, roads, or buildings. Did somebody actually think they were 'designing' answers in this kit, or were the answers simply 'provided'?

"He has *served as* president of the organization in the last year." Better: "He was the organization's president in the last year." In the first sentence, it seems as if we are implying this person merely pretended to act as if he was president, when indeed he really was not president. (Perhaps an interim, filling an unexpired term?) But in fact, he either was or he wasn't president — so why beat around the bush? You've also reduced a twelve-word sentence to nine words, too.

Are you contributing to the barrage of tired, overworked, repetitious phrases that creep into religious literature, confounding those of us who are trying to read you on a sixth grade level? Begin with these five linguistic atrocities — *that, new, special, designed to, served as* — in a personal quest to break down your own language barriers.

"My five infamous friends" were introduced to the readers of a denominational publication awhile back. Some interesting letters to the editor followed. This one was typical.*

> I want to thank James Cox for *that new* approach *that* is *designed to serve as that* corrective in our *special* articles in the *new* denominational publications *designed to* speak to *special* age groups like singles, marrieds, parents, children, old folks, and young folks, *that serve as* curriculum supplements to our regular literature *that* is normally

*From *The Baptist Program*, June/July 1979. © Copyright 1979 Executive Committee of the Southern Baptist Convention. All rights reserved. Used by permission.

> *designed to serve as* the core for the *special* continuing programs of our always *new* Southern Baptist churches.
>
> So far I have not yet become a *special* writer *that* would write something *that* would be worth *special* enough note *that* it would meet the *new* criteria our editors may have adopted *that* are *designed to serve as* guidelines in hereafter published writings. But if the day comes I will always be grateful for the introduction Mr. Cox gave me to his friends. They are now my *special new* friends *that* I hope will *serve as* faithful companions *designed to* help me become a "would-be writer."

Perhaps the letter writer missed something along the way. But I am indebted to him at any rate for pointing out yet another bit of denominational jargon in the process.

Did you notice he used the term *speak to*? I could not count the times I have read articles by professional religious leaders in which they used sentences such as, "This program will *speak to* the needs of children in grades one through six." Why can't the program *answer* those needs? Have you ever heard a program/book/resource kit/curriculum piece/conference/leaflet/survey/report/etc. ad infinitum verbally *speak* to anything? It might offer information, but without human qualities, a program just does not audibly *speak*. What's wrong with calling a spade a spade?

Some Also Rans

We have considered some of the worst offenders in a freelancer's manuscripts. But these culprits don't stand alone. If "my five infamous friends" are rated almost fatal, the following result at least in cardiac arrests when used in overdose proportions:

the
of
on
and

Consider these examples.

"He is *the* minister of *the* First Presbyterian Church, Centerville." Better: "He is minister of First Presbyterian Church, Centerville." The definite article is not required to be clearly understood. The extra words contribute no further meaning but do consume extra space.

"The award was given to Randall Green *of* Burbank *of* Los Angeles Diocese for his significant contributions." Better: "The award was given to Randall Green, Burbank, Los Angeles Diocese, for his significant contributions." Although *of* might be used in verbal speech, commas often allow you to delete *of* when writing. There can be no doubt about your meaning as written here.

"He will run the mile *on* Friday, unless it is raining, in which case he will run *on* Saturday." Better: "He will run the mile Friday, unless it is raining, in which case he will run Saturday." What does *on* contribute to the meaning of this sentence? Obviously nothing. So why use it?

"We are going to the store *and* then on to town *and* by my brother's house *and* sooner or later we will get to your house." Better: "We are going first to the store, then to town. We'll stop by my brother's house next. Eventually we'll get to yours." Robert Gunning would love you if you learn to split one twenty-six word sentence into three shorter ones of twenty-two words combined, without losing any of the original meaning! You can separate many words and clauses you normally connect with *and* by breaking them into shorter sentences (bite-sized portions), or by adding punctuation marks — most frequently commas and semicolons.

Each writer will have to think all of this through for himself, of course. In the end, an editor will have the final say over all of our divergent opinions. The style manual he ascribes to is the ultimate authority, no matter how strong our personal convictions. Be prepared to accept his judgment in this and all other writing endeavors if you are serious about wanting to be published.

There are a few other things which bug me in choosing words which others will read. Variety is the spice of life, and a writer's copy acquires extra sparkle when it includes different terms rather than the same one again and again. For example, have you ever thought about the word *said*, and how many hundreds of substitutes there are for it?

Once upon a time, I knew a writer who used *said* before or after every quote of every speaker in every story he wrote. There was almost never any variation at all. Yet, it would have been just as simple for him to have selected words as these to bring new life to his copy:

mused	*pondered*
declared	*cried*

intoned | *scolded*
exclaimed | *interrupted*
laughed | *chided*
reasoned | *suggested*
implored | *promised*
figured | *demanded*
pled | *underscored*
questioned | *revealed*

These are action words, and they tell us something of the subject's own personal demeanor while speaking. To state, " 'Bring that book here!' he said" is not nearly as forceful, colorful, or descriptive as, " 'Bring that book here!' he demanded." If you have fallen into the trap of relying on *said* — or any other one word, to the exclusion of all others with similar meanings — your copy is probably suffering from the blahs. Look for creative and unusual action words which can add zest to your manuscripts.

By the way, if you would like to try an interesting experiment, ask a group of people (writers, or others) to jot down as many substitutes for the word *said* as they can think of within fifteen minutes. The winner will be the one with the longest list. You may be surprised how many different ways of saying *said* your guests can derive. Their lists may also be an invaluable resource to you later when you need *said* substitutes for your manuscripts.

Trim Away the Fat

While you're playing games, you might also like to try this little experiment on a group of friends or by yourself. It's an exercise I once used in a classroom setting with beginning writers. See if you can economize the expressions and sentences used here. Answers are at the end of the chapter, but you'll get more out of it (and enjoy it more) if you don't peek first. More than one possible answer exists for many questions, but only one answer is required.

A. Compress the following statements into *one* word:

Example: *at that time* Answer: *then* or *when*

1. on one occasion ______
2. a small number of ______
3. in addition to ______
4. in the near future ______

5. any one of the two ____________
6. at the present time ____________
7. all of a sudden ____________
8. once in a great while ____________
9. in the same manner as ____________
10. a large number of ____________
11. at regular intervals of time ____________
12. tendered his resignation ____________
13. taken to jail and locked up ____________
14. was able to make his escape ____________
15. brought to a sudden halt ____________

B. Delete all unnecessary words:

Example: *lift it up* Answer: *lift*

1. in a dying condition ____________
2. first of all ____________
3. he continued on ____________
4. his final conclusion ____________
5. a pregnant Cuban woman ____________
6. during the course of the day ____________
7. a bald-headed man ____________
8. skirted around obstacles ____________
9. set a new record ____________
10. cannot possibly be ____________
11. wearing a happy smile on her face ____________
12. throughout the entire day ____________
13. assembled crowd of people ____________
14. attended by fifty invited guests ____________

15. established traditions of the past ________________
16. was killed when a fatal bullet ________________
17. car was completely destroyed ________________
18. a small size woman ________________
19. in the city of Minneapolis ________________
20. for a short space of time ________________

C. **Rewrite more concisely:**

1. We came to a decision to allow him to go.

2. I asked him about possible problems that might arise.

3. A second suggestion that I would offer is that we might ...

4. In these past five years from that day ...

5. Perhaps some of the answers which I discovered through my own experience will encourage others.

6. It was with a show of emotion that he said ...

7. She lived in the city of Birmingham in the state of Alabama.

____

____

8. It is an actual fact that the government of this city ended up by expending monetary funds totaling the sum of $500,000 in the year that has just passed.

____

____

9. The unforeseen accident took place all of a sudden at the corner of Fourth Street and Broadway Street when the two vehicles crashed into each other.

____

____

10. She put in her appearance at the hour of noon.

____

____

I am indebted to my good friend Lucien E. Coleman, professor of religious education at Southern Baptist Theological Seminary, Louisville, Kentucky, for providing much of the material included in the above exercise.

There are many, many good books on grammar available to anyone desiring help. (A few are listed in the appendix at the back of this book.) Basically, however, the freelancer must have an intuitive ability to choose the right word. He should also be acquainted with any peculiarities in style which the publication for which he intends to write may have. Some editors, church publications, and/or religious publishing houses issue their own style manuals which help their writers maintain uniformity. You might inquire if such is available if you plan to do a lot of writing for one individual, periodical, or publisher.

Once again, a study of back issues of the magazines will often provide you with some clues on whether to call Bible study 'Sunday School,' 'Church School,' or by some other name for a particular denomination; whether to spell *enrolment* with one 'l' or two; whether to indent all paragraphs or not; and whether to use commas before *and* in a series of three or more items, such as "She had eggs, bacon, and toast." (We don't use those commas on our paper, but many religious editors still do.)

"My five infamous friends" — and other maladies of the writing profession — may soon begin to bug the life out of you, just like they do me. If they do, you will have begun to lay some foundations toward becoming a better writer, the kind that eventually sees his work appearing in print.

The scriptures affirm, "What a joy it is to find just the right word for the right occasion!" (Prov. 15:23, TEV). A writer realizes the truth of that verse as much as anybody.

And now, for the answers to the economy in writing quiz:

Check Yourself Out

A.

1. once, when
2. few
3. also, besides, additionally, plus, and
4. soon, shortly, momentarily
5. either, one
6. now, today, presently, currently, nowadays
7. suddenly, abruptly, unexpectedly
8. infrequently, seldom, occasionally
9. like, similarly, likewise, correspondingly, similar, alike
10. many, numerous, lots
11. frequently, often, repeatedly, periodically
12. resigned, quit, terminated
13. jailed, incarcerated, imprisoned, impounded, arrested
14. escaped, fled
15. stopped, halted

B.

1. dying
2. first
3. he continued
4. his conclusion
5. a pregnant Cuban
6. during the day
7. a bald man
8. skirted obstacles
9. set a record

10. cannot be
11. wearing a smile
12. through the day
13. crowd
14. attended by fifty guests
15. established traditions
16. was killed when a bullet
17. car was destroyed
18. a small woman
19. in Minneapolis
20. for a short time

C.

(Note: Other possible answers exist for this portion of the exercise. These are *examples* of answers.)

1. We decided to let him go.
2. I asked him about possible problems.
3. A second suggestion is to ...
4. In the five years since ...
5. Perhaps my own findings will help others.
6. Emotionally, he said ...
7. She lived in Birmingham, Ala.
8. In the year just ended, this city spent $500,000.
9. The accident occurred at Fourth and Broadway when two vehicles collided.
10. She arrived at noon.

Scoring: In part A, count three points for each correct answer; in part B, count two points for each correct answer; and in part C, count 1½ points for each answer written about as concisely as it could possibly be. A perfect score is 100.

4
Where Do You Get Such Ideas?

Solicited testimonials from prolific freelancers

I've already had my say on developing a system of writing which is uniquely the writer's own. I've told you what has worked for me and what hasn't, and even hinted I could wallpaper a nice-sized room with the rejection slips I've acquired over a couple of decades. I told you how I launched my avocational freelancing career, and the kind of article that is easiest for me to write.

Lest I delude you into thinking there's one preset formula for success in writing, let me hasten to add I've consulted nine other freelancers in the church market to gain wider perspectives. (Secretly, I really wanted to know what made them so successful so I could beg, borrow, or steal their ideas!)

Seriously, I do believe they can contribute some suggestions worth considering by the aspiring freelancer. While I value the judgment of each one highly, again let me caution you — just as I did when I spelled out my own writing system — what works for them may not work for you. Keep that in mind as you read their suggestions. Be yourself, and adapt and modify every successful freelancer's sacred 'laws' only as they work for you.

To conduct this little experiment, I devised a 10-question survey form which inquired some things I felt both the novice and the experienced writer could profit from. I'm not going to try to share *every* writer's answer to *every* question — some of it isn't totally relevant — but I shall give you the highlights of what was said. I will state a question exactly as the freelancers were given it, then offer a sampling of their answers. In this way you can have the benefit of comparing what was said.

1. What's the Best Time of Day for You to Write?

We've mentioned this subject before for it does seem to have some effect on a writer's quality of work and on the quantity of copy he is able to produce. Finding one's own time that is conducive to good writing is the objective.

Not all those surveyed on this subject agree with one another. One, for instance, a religious editor as well as a freelancer, was adamant in his belief "a skilled writer could discipline himself to write at all hours. It's a myth to think there's a 'certain time.' " He also admitted he preferred morning as a time to write.

A syndicated newspaper columnist apparently sided with him.

"Truthfully, I can write at any time," he said. "Because of my schedule I write whenever I get the time." This writer indicated he mostly preferred evenings for writing, however.

All other participants in the survey were explicit about their writing time, with morning hours (even early morning hours) favored by more than half. Typical responses:

From a mother of preschoolers — "With small children, I find my *only* quiet time to be early morning. However, as I get older, I find it more difficult to heed the alarm clock!"

From a seminary professor—"Morning. Between 8:00 and 12:00 noon. I'm not much good in early morning hours, like 5:00, and energy is low in afternoon."

Because of their employment, at least two respondents could not write in the mornings. One said his most fruitful writing is done on Saturdays. Another opted for evenings and weekends.

2. Do You Have a Favorite Place to Write?

The writer who said there's no such thing as a "certain time" to do good work also labeled this idea as "another myth." He scoffed at the premise a "secret hideway by the beach or in the woods will guarantee success."

Another said he is capable of writing "in airports, schools, lawns, streets."

With the exception of these, and another who writes exclusively at his office in non-working hours, average writers apparently do require that "secret hideaway," however. Most have an office, a desk or a private nook at home in which they grind out reams of manuscript pages over short periods of time.

"I think a writer must have a special place that is always available to him," said a mother who also serves in a full time church staff capacity. "I have a large desk with good lighting, with filing cabinets and book shelves at easy reach. I enjoy being close to my family when I write, so my desk is in the family room."

Interestingly, at least to me, none of those surveyed argued for writing out-of-doors. Somehow, nature attracts me, and I occasionally write in longhand in a lawn chair or hammock under the trees on yellow legal pads. I type what I've written later indoors (when the sun has gone down, or when it's raining). I'm beginning to wonder if I'm the only scribe who likes to write under blue skies and golden sun!

3. How Did You Get Started Freelancing?

As you might expect, my nine counterparts each had a different story to tell.

One was invited to write a series of articles for a church publication and became convinced "I could write for publication." A journalism course helped him develop the urge to write for print, and he plunged in.

A teacher was the catalyst that prompted another freelancer to give it her best shot after the instructor had read some of her work.

Another was inspired as a child by Sherwood Wirt's *Winesburg, Ohio*, so he began a daily journal. One thing led to another and eventually a local paper published some of his articles. Today his own weekly syndicated column appears in more than 300 secular papers around the globe, and he also writes profusely for the church market.

Finally, yet another said, "I have *always* wanted to be a writer." Approached about writing lesson courses for her church's periodicals, she "simply took a deep breath and began submitting books and articles." Nowadays, it seems almost every time I pick up a magazine from her denomination, I find her name listed among the bylines.

If you took 100 successful freelancers and asked them how they started, you'd probably get 90 or 95 and perhaps even 100 different answers. That suggests to me the important thing is now *how* you start, but *that* you start.

4. What Type of Material Is Easiest for You to Write?

I had hoped we might prove something here, and I guess we did, but it wasn't what I had anticipated. I had hoped to say most writers participating in this survey clearly favor poetry, or fiction, or meditations, or whatever — anything — it didn't really matter. But, once again, they professed no obvious favorites, thereby proving you can be a successful freelancer in the church market in a wide variety of areas.

Three of the respondents mentioned 'personal experience articles' as their preferences while two suggested 'fiction.' Also included at least once were these: teaching procedures, devotional material, humor, Bible stories, poetry, interviews, nostalgia, personality profiles, pastoral, religious, informative, and nonfiction.

So, take your pick. If you've got the gift, obviously you can be successful in more than one writing field in religious freelancing.

5. Where Do You Find Ideas for Stories and Articles?

(You will note this is the question which prompted this chapter's title.)

"I find ideas everywhere I go," declared one writer. "I am careful to write them down before I forget them. I keep files of examples and true life incidents to begin articles and stories, ideas for future books, and articles."

This was a typical answer. Not surprisingly, more than half the respondents declared 'personal experience,' 'encounter,' or 'observation' was the basis of a great many articles they produce. One reported: "Most of my stuff is related to religious experience, to church programs and the like. It's not uncommon to be struggling with a problem and say, 'Hey, I'm not the only one that struggles with this kind of problem.' "

At least four of the nine writers mentioned a wide variety of reading materials as primary sources for article ideas, too. A couple relied almost altogether on books, magazines, and newspapers for "a word or phrase" which is the germ of a later article idea.

Two other writers answered the question with "all sorts of places" and "everywhere," which could indicate a heavy leaning on personal experience and/or reading matter.

Obviously, the ideas are out there. The prolific freelancer has to be observant and have the ability to decide what in his experience will make a good story which others will want to read. Perhaps that's as much a sixth sense as anything else.

6. Do You Concentrate on Certain Markets, Editors, or Magazines? Why?

All of those interviewed indicated they concentrated heavily on their own church's printed materials, probably first and foremost for the security and repeat sales this market generates for them. They are also obviously familiar with what's available here.

One pointed out, however, she was surely "open to other markets."

A religious editor said he relied on his church's periodicals as a freelancer for two reasons: a "limited amount of discretionary time" in which to write avocationally, and because "I know the target better."

Another explained somewhat facetiously, "Because my daddy taught me years ago to keep fishing a crappie hole where they were still biting." Less cryptically, he acknowledged, "I can sell everything I have time to write to this market," so — in effect — why not?

A professional childhood education leader for a religious organization said she concentrated primarily on child-related materials for church publications. "That's the area I know best, and a form of ministry for me," she averred.

One respondent listed specific church magazines on which he depended. He favored one in particular for its "saturation of clergy"; others, for their appeal to large audiences, and so on.

Finally, another twist was introduced by a writer who stated she concentrated on certain editors she enjoyed working with.

"Every good writer needs a good editor," she explained, "so I am selective in deciding where I will send a manuscript."

I believe she is quite right, and will have more to say about this in the next chapter.

Many successful freelancers for religious publications eventually learn what markets want the kind of material they specialize in, and concentrate their efforts there.

I once worked for an employer whose operating philosophy was, "Just because something has always pulled well for you, why continue it?"

Because, my friend, when you buy a ticket to ride a train, you don't get off until your coach reaches your destination.

The same with writing. Why jump board for lots of uncertainties and insecurities when you get lots more dependable mileage (and acceptance checks) from the gravy train you've already boarded?

Find the places — periodicals, editors, subjects — which provide a base of guaranteed sales security for you, even as you may experiment with other innovative ideas elsewhere, and respect it as your bread and butter. Concentrate at least fifty percent of your efforts there. This idea has worked for so many others before, why can't it provide an almost guaranteed income for you?

7. How Do You Handle Rejection Slips?

These points may be summarized in this phrase: *Successful freelancers never let their rejections dissuade them.*

"I used to take it personally," said one hack. "Not any more."

When question seven was posed, another replied, "So what?"

A third acknowledged, "I put them in the wastebasket."

Still another: "I accept them as part of the writing process." He added that rejection slips angered him if he felt "the editor didn't read my submission."

One survey participant shocked this writer by stating he wouldn't know how to act with a rejection slip because in perhaps three decades of freelancing he had never received one! (He told me later this is the gospel truth. He's the *only* successful freelancer this author ever knew so blessed, so don't anticipate history to repeat itself.)

I liked the fact several mentioned they didn't give up easily when a submitted manuscript was rejected by an editor.

"I never assume it's worthless," said one. "If I have a good feeling about a manuscript, I will send it to several publishers before giving up." (Recall the earlier advice about never throwing anything away.)

Finally, one beautifully summarized: "My rejections keep me humble; my acceptances keep me writing."

Perhaps we all need an occasional rejection slip to help us properly appreciate this gift of God, and to bring us added joy when we do make a sale.

8. What Are the Satisfactions You Derive from Writing?

There were basically six answers to this question. Not all of them could be classified as altogether altruistic.

Four persons enjoy helping or influencing others. Said one, "I especially gain satisfaction from letters I receive from people who are helped by my writing. I keep and treasure every letter."

Another indicated this was her opportunity "to witness, to bless, and to inspire others."

Three found freelancing self-fulfilling in some measure, one admitting he enjoyed seeing his name in print.

A pastor's wife said writing was "an outlet, therapy, unequaled expression which means a great deal to my identity."

Two answers received two votes each — use of a specialized talent, and monetary reward.

One freelancer recognized she possesses "a highly developed skill which only a limited number of persons have." She felt compelled to use it, recognizing it as a very sacred trust from the Creator.

On remuneration, a prolific writer admitted, "I make more money from my writing 'hobby' than from my career as a full time church staff member." (This scribe finds this statement difficult to comprehend — the freelancer is either tremendously talented, zealously dedicated, notoriously fibbing, poor in mathematics, or all four; or this is a tremendous indictment on what we're paying our church employes these days!)

Finally, there was one vote cast for doing God's will and one for the satisfaction of personal study, preparation, and discipline.

You may have other reasons for writing, or for wanting to write, but these answers are among those many writers for church publications often offer first. Do any of them sound familiar?

9. What Are Some Things a Freelancer Needs to Know in Order To Be Successful in Writing?

Without comment, here's what one said:

1. Know how to use the English language, clearly and accurately.
2. Know the publications you write for, and their audiences.
3. Know what you're talking about. There are only two excuses for writing an article. Either you know more about the subject than the reader does, or you can say it entertainingly. If you don't know your subject, you've got to find out the hard way — through research.

Another:

1. Know one's audience.
2. Know the language (grammar/style).
3. Know you have something to say.

4. Be gutsy enough to think someone wants to hear what you have to say.

Still another:

1. Know what sort of articles or books a particular publisher looks for. It is doubtful that the publisher will change his publishing plans no matter how marvelous your manuscript may be.
2. Know the approximate length of articles a magazine prints.
3. Study the writing style of a magazine. You will have to adjust your style to fit the magazine's style or find a magazine that has a similar style to yours.

Langauge, market, subject. Master these three areas and you're on your way to a start in freelancing, according to the experts.

10. What Advice Would You Give Someone Just Starting Out in Freelancing?

How about these good pointers from the successful newspaper columnist and religious freelancer?

1. Don't give up; persistence pays off!
2. Read everything you can.
3. Study people: their emotions, etc.
4. Study writing styles of prominent authors.
5. Know editors' needs.
6. Study the markets.
7. Read professional manuals.
8. Talk to other writers.
9. Attend writing seminars.
10. Pray for guidance.
11. Try to really experience life.
12. Observe details.
13. Write, write, write.
14. Spend some time alone.

The man who offered these suggestions added, "Writing is an obsession with me. I have no choice but to write. It is not something I *want* to do more than it is what I *must* do."

If that expression sums up your commitment, too, perhaps the advice my fellow freelancers in the church market have shared on their pilgrimages to success will give you some new perspectives from which to put down your thoughts.

5

Have You a Friend in the Diamond Business?

The editors demand (and get) equal time

At a banquet table around which a number of religious editors sat several years ago, I heard a speaker — himself an ordained minister — relate a story of a certain preacher who had died.

Arriving at the Pearly Gates, the man identified himself to St. Peter, who in turn checked the master list of names he kept nearby.

When the preacher's name was found, the gates swung open and he was waved inside. No fanfare accompanied his arrival, but then the clergyman did not really expect notoriety, either.

Momentarily, an editor also arrived at the gates, and he, too, was checked against the master list. When his name was also found there, the gates subsequently parted and he, too, was motioned inside.

Just then a strange thing happened. Great shouts went up among the mortals present, and angels began singing in chorus. Not only that, carillons chimed, bells rang, organs played, trumpets sounded, harps were heard, and the heavenly hosts rejoiced exceedingly and flocked to the editor's side.

It was absolutely more than the man of the cloth, who stood by speechless looking on, could bear. There must be some explanation for this unusual outburst for a mere layman, thought he, when there was no noticeable expression for a preacher's arrival. He returned to St. Peter and inquired into the perplexing dilemma.

With a twinkle in his eye, St. Peter was quick to set the minister straight.

"Ah," said he. "Do not fret. You see, in these parts, preachers are a dime a dozen. But we don't get very many editors in here!"

There are words for people like that (editors). Here are a few of the most descriptive I can think of for those I've known and written for:

objective	*knowledgeable*
educated	*scholarly*
temperamental	*stubborn*
forgiving	*considerate*
God-fearing	*anxious*
perfectionist	*dedicated*
humorous	*merciless*
sensitive	*flexible*
determined	*egotistical*
capable	*successful*

Before giving a misleading impression, let me explain I recall only two of the couple of hundred I've written for in the church market that could be classified pure egotists. (Neither is still an editor, by the way.) Most who were temperamental or stubborn or merciless usually showed that side only when it came to deadlines, not bad virtues for editors *or* freelancers.

Awhile back, I penned a few reverential lines for those slave-drivers whom writers call editors. With tongue in cheek, I am happy to share them with you here.

Behold the Editor!

Behold the editor, that unsung yet beleagured hero of the printed page! While others pursue fame and fortune, his sole claim to fame consists of his name appearing in eight point type on some nameless publication's masthead.

Daily he presides over a desk situated precisely in the middle of a barrage of crossfires shot from cannons which strangely enough resemble intercoms, telephones, typewriters, Xerox machines, dictaphones, memo pads, in-baskets, mail boxes, and very big mouths.

The editor is hounded on all sides. Some of his most fearless detractors include persnickity publishers, all-knowing artists, pokey printers, peculiar proofreaders, and scurrilious subscribers, to say nothing of vacationing visitors who drop by his office for a minute and remain for hours.

Add to these a rather heavy assortment of wretched writers who submit poorly written and underresearched manuscripts; who murder the King's English; who don't know the meaning of deadlines; who are out of touch with the demographics of the publication's audience for whom they are writing; and who expect to be paid more than their material could ever be worth if it was submitted on the back side of the original Mona Lisa. What have you got?

An editor with any or all of the following symptoms, sometimes simultaneously: bulging eyeballs; buzzing ears; palpitations of the heart; fidgets of the lower extremities; facial contortions; loss of hearing, vision, speech, hair, teeth, and appetite; acne; dizziness; indigestion; ulcers; irregularity; nervous and emotional disorders; insomnia; overweight; aches and pains of unknown origin; and an affinity for writers' cramp.

On top of that, the editor laughs all the way to the bank — not because he is overcompensated, but because he anticipates the look on his banker's face as he applies for a loan to fill the gas tank of his '63 Ford.

His hate mail from irate readers introduces his vocabulary to words he never knew existed as he scurries to the dictionary in search of their meaning. Fortunately, he can't find all of them.

Yet, when there is praise for an article in the magazine which he edits, the writer receives it, no matter how good the editor made that half-baked story sound.

When someone comments on the attractiveness of the periodical, the designer takes a bow.

When no errors are found, the proofreader is commended.

And when the publication wins a national award, the publisher shows up to receive it.

Is there no mercy and justice in this world? Ah, yes, behold the editor! He, too, shall have his piece of the rock, albeit merely a cinder to be trodden over by some freelancer traveling up the road to success.

Faith, Hope, and Hilarity

Those who edit church publications are pretty decent sorts, I've found. They have ambitions and goals and dreams just like their writers. They have to succeed in order to provide a living for their families, too. They work within approved guidelines and frameworks and sometimes fool with a lot of red tape they would rather disregard, but such decisions are often made by management personnel.

Most editors are patient and kind, just like the thirteenth chapter of First Corinthians admonishes, and are sensitive to the needs and concerns of their writers. They are occasionally willing to go out on a limb to let an inexperienced writer try his wings, and they often encourage writers to be creative and explore virgin territory, within bounds. Most have that perfectionist aura about them (just as many successful freelancers do), most have a good sense of humor, and most are well prepared through education and experience for their jobs. Finally, my belief is that most of them love the Lord and experience a daily walk with him.

Obviously, if they weren't succeeding as an editor, they would have been removed long ago by the publisher or a supervising manager.

I've had my share of 'run-ins' with editors. I've told you already about one or two. Another one told me quite frankly my writing was never going to amount to anything if I didn't get my Fog Index a lot lower than it was. (For those of you who may not understand that term, it's Gunning's system for gauging the educational level of the readers for whom one writes. The Bible, for instance, usually is easy reading for those who have completed sixth or seventh grade.)

This editor complained my level of writing was frequently pitched to an audience with sixteen or more years of schooling. She was right, I found out, and I've never forgotten that advice, although it was tough hearing it at the time.

I would judge at least ninety-five percent of my encounters with editors have been pleasant ones, however. Although some rejected manuscripts I was convinced the world was waiting for, they often did so in such a way I felt like thanking them for the beautifully written turn-downs! They encouraged me, helped me regain confidence after a long dry spell, saw strengths in my writing which were oblivious to me, and often accepted as submitted manuscripts I wish I had spent more time on.

In Louisville, Kentucky, there is a jeweler whose slogan has been repeated so frequently on the airwaves and in the print media Louisvillians have come to associate it immediately with the company it represents. This is exactly what the ad agency that developed it wants, of course. But I think the slogan makes a point which is worth considering here. The slogan reads, *Now you have a friend in the diamond business.*

For those of us who produce pretty rough copy sometimes, we need somebody to run 'roughshod' on us, yet do it in a gentle manner. In my thinking, a writer's very best friend in this business can be his editor. Editors can turn disappointments into opportunities, weaknesses into wealth, rejects into gems, and help a dull hack polish up his act and make it shine.

He can go to bat for you when a reader raises a question about something you've written. He can take a chance on an unknown quantity when the aspiring writer is trying desperately to break into print. He can believe in his writers' ability and dependability enough to make assignments to them. He relies on his regular writers to get the proper facts and put them together in an acceptable manner. He counts on his writers to make contributions to his publication which will be interesting, entertaining, and stimulating to his readers. And he often encourager 'hose writers when they are experiencing a kind of writing slump.

Frankly, discovering a good editor, and maintaining his good will, is one of the most satisfying rewards that ever comes to a freelancer.

An editor once patiently took the trouble to write me a lot of detailed instructions about what he was looking for in manuscripts, his peculiar style requirements, and so on, then apologized: "I am taking your time and mine, too, in this endeavor because I feel like it is the beginning of a writer-editor relationship that will result in other articles in the future." It was, and it did. I heard him loud and clear, and tried to follow his instructions. As a result I've been asked to write for him again and again.

Don't be incensed if an editor asks for a rewrite, or suggests how he would like for you to improve or alter a piece you have submitted for his publication. (A couple of times, in lengthy curriculum assignments, I have been unable to make extensive revisions an editor requested due to a lack of available time. But this is an exception rather than a rule, and should be avoided if at all possible.)

Accept the words of experience which come from your editors and seek to provide copy exactly as they request it, provided it does not compromise principles, beliefs, or theology you hold sacred. We've already observed there's nothing to be gained — *ever* — in getting mad at an editor. If you react in a manner unbecoming a professional, word may get around to other editors, and some of your potential markets may be diminished.

Advice from the Type Worn

In the previous chapter, some very successful freelancers in the church market shared their success stories with you. Now I'd like to let some editors of denominational publications get in their words of advice, too.

As I was preparing to lead a series of writers' conferences not so long ago, I surveyed sixteen editors of church magazines on a number of subjects. You might be interested in some of the generalizations which came out of this study:

- Every editor contacted said at least some portion, usually fifty percent or more, of each issue of the magazine he edits is produced by assignment. In other words, the editor of every church publication participating in this survey seeks specific writers to provide copy on topics the editor has previously selected for treatment in the magazine, or topics suggested by a writer which are approved before the writer's final copy is submitted. The remainder of the magazine (usually less than half) is by freelance submission.
- At least a dozen of these 16 editors (75%) indicated it was not necessary for a writer to query them before sending in an article. (But if you're going to do a lot of research or expect to put in many long hours on an article, my suggestion is to first ask the editor about his interest in it before you go to all that trouble.)
- The 'lead time' before a submission appears in print from the time it is accepted ranges from two months in one periodical to twelve months or more in others. For curriculum, the 'lead time' often ranges up to three years from the time a writer accepts an assignment until he sees his work in print.
- About half of those editors interviewed said if time permits and a manuscript revision is necessary, the writer is usually requested to make the changes. Otherwise, someone on the editorial staff or another outsider paid by the publication revises the material according to the editor's wishes.

Here are a couple of direct questions asked of the editors participating in the survey, and their answers:

1. What are some reasons a manuscript may be unacceptable?

Interestingly, of sixteen editors responding, ten arrived at the same conclusion: "Weak in writing ability."

Editors were permitted to give as many reasons why a manuscript might be unacceptable as they wished, but this one item was readily named by the majority.

Other answers given for refusing a writers' work included these:

"Subject unsuitable" — five responses

"Doesn't fit the audience" — five responses

"Weak in content" — three responses

"Subject covered in a recent article" — three responses

"Unacceptable teaching philosophy and methods" — three responses

There were other causes, such as "Sounds like a sermon," "Not written on assignment," "Not written according to specifications," "Belaboring the obvious," "Not believable," "Too pious," "Too long," "Gives the 'I've read this 1000 times before' feeling," "Not familiar with materials writing about," and "Christian perspective omitted."

I was surprised that weakness in writing ability topped the list, but then, I had falsely assumed most manuscripts editors receive come from people who use the Mother Tongue correctly, and who have some flair for writing. If grammar is your weakness, you can get help. But if a lack of talent is your albatross, better pick another hobby for this one is an exacting field and to be successful in it you can't be an amateur for very long.

Most of the other problem areas could have been reduced if writers had known the market, the publications, editors, and audiences for whom they were writing. Of course, they need a good grasp of the subject they are writing about, they need to follow style rules, and they need the good fortune of submitting an article at just the right time in the right market. A little of this is guesswork, but a whole lot is in being familiar with what you have to say, who will read it, and having the ability to communicate it interestingly.

2. What suggestions would you give aspiring writers for your publication?

Five editors answered: "Be familiar with the publication and material used." (There! We've said it, repeatedly, again!)

Four added: "Know methodology and philosophy." (You can't communicate something you don't first understand yourself.)

Four more suggested: "Be creative — include warmth and humanity." (Make your ideas and copy sparkle and interest the reader.)

Three concurred: "Consider what our readers need and want to know." (After all, we *are* in business to serve a constituency. It *does* matter what the subscriber's needs are.)

Three others declared: "Be thorough in research." (Don't leave anything to chance, and document carefully what you find and use.)

Two directed: "Use a good idea — have something to say." (If not, be prepared to fold up your tent and move quietly to the outskirts of town!)

Two also commented: "Don't be scholarly." (Remember the old Fog Index routine? I can testify, it's no laughing matter.)

Two more admonished: "Rewrite, edit, rewrite, and rewrite again." (Now, have you ever heard that before?)

There are some other suggestions: "Include fact and feeling," "Be clear and logical," and "Don't preach."

Good advice for the novice and the experienced journalist as well.

Recently, Robert J. Hastings, editor of the Illinois Baptist, weekly newspaper published in Springfield, Illinois, shared with me the kind of material he desired for his publication. I've asked for the privilege of passing it along for it gives some insights into how one editor views his role and identifies the audience he is attempting to serve:

> When I put the Illinois Baptist together, I try to visualize, say, an Illinois farmer coming in at dinnertime from planting soybeans. He looks over our paper, and what interests him?
>
> What interests him (or any reader) is what he identifies with. A newspaper is a mirror, and when a reader sees himself reflected therein, his interest is immediate.
>
> The soybean farmer is not too interested in denominational machinery, awards, plaques, dignitaries, and the like.
>
> But he is interested — and I believe impressed — when he sees himself, his church, his interests — mirrored in what denominational agencies are doing.

Is there a soybean farmer you can visualize out there reading the magazine you hope to write for? Or a preacher? Or a church school teacher? Or an elder? Or a young person?

Your friend, the editor, can help you get a better grasp on who you need to pitch your material toward, after you've first won his confidence in your ability. He can suggest certain slants to take, and provide you with subjects that are appropriate to the needs and interests of the audience for whom you are writing.

Cultivate his friendship. In fact, try to develop several sustaining writer-editor relationships. The result may be lots more acceptances and lots fewer rejections of your freelance submissions.

An editor cuts, hones, polishes, and smoothes out the wrinkles in a writer's copy to allow that writer's words to shine. He doesn't get much credit for what he does, but the luster and sparkle turns up on the printed page just the same.

Have you a friend in the diamond business?

6

The Opera Ain't Over 'Til the Fat Lady Sings

From rough draft to finished craft

Do you like to play games? I hope so, for I've got one I'd like for you to play with me right now. It's a pretend game, and I hope you'll put yourself into the role of being my pretend friend for just a moment. Are you ready?

Here's what I want you to do:

1. Pretend you've got a fantastic new slant for an article on a controversial topic currently being bantered about by the religious community. Got that?

2. Now, pretend to determine the market/audience you will shoot for, and the periodical you will slant your story toward.

3. Then, pretend to investigate the subject thoroughly. You will check out published references on it, interview others to determine what they have to say about the subject, and gather an extensive amount of data to be drawn upon as you write.

4. Finally, after absorbing as much of the research as you can, pretend to write a very timely, thoughtful, objective, and informative piece which an editor will want for his publication.

5. Now, stop and think. Is there anything else you should give consideration to before the editor receives your manuscript?

In previous chapters, we've offered some tricks of the trade which have worked not only for the author but for some of his free-lancing buddies, too. We've discussed the importance of developing one's own personal writing system. We've examined the road to more effective communication through cleaner copy.

And, some editors in the church market have even shared their personal gripes about manuscripts.

Have we covered the waterfront? Well, not quite yet. Someone has aptly remarked, "The opera ain't over 'til the fat lady sings."

All the inside tips and helpful advice on how to write a story for sale is of little consequence if a writer can't get a sympathetic reading of that story by an editor or a member of his staff. And so many times, the thing that separates the two is the appearance of the copy which the writer submits to an editor.

For a moment, let's carry our pretend game a little further. Let's suppose you are an editor of a widely circulated religious magazine. One day at the top of the stack of your morning mail you find an unsolicited manuscript of the following description:

Dog-eared, it's typed using an obviously worn ribbon on light cream-colored stock. While this distinguishes it immediately from the host of other manuscripts vying for the editor's attention, it tends to enhance the spilled coffee stains and fingerprint smudges the author has also submitted. He didn't think too much about margins, either, for there practically aren't any. He forgot to number his pages. While most of the material was double spaced, at the bottom of some pages he squeezed in an extra line or two. To top it all off, the editor received it: "Postage Due 13 Cents."

Are you still pretending with me? If so, what do you think you would do with this manuscript?

I suspect you'd do the same thing I would: reach for a preprinted rejection slip, attach it to the manuscript, and place it in your out-basket for a secretary to pick up and return to the sender later in the day.

In fact, if I were the editor, unless I was absolutely desperate for a piece right then on the subject the writer offered, I'd never read the first graph. My time would be too valuable to waste on such tripe. I would have already surmised, if the writer's work *looks* this bad, it must surely *be* this bad! After all, he obviously took no pains to make me *want* to read it — what do I owe him?

Everything You Needed to Know, but Didn't Know Whom to Ask

What do you need to know to get your material into acceptable shape so it stands at least a competing chance of being read by somebody on the editorial staff?

There are lots of things you can do, and we'll attempt to cover a great number of them in this chapter. There are at least five which are absolutely essential. I call them the "Five Cardinal Rules of Manuscript Preparation." Break any one of them and you do irreparable harm to the finished product, no matter how good it may be.

In fact, it is doubtful the negative side effects caused by violating these can be offset by the positive effects of a good manuscript. Even if the editor reads it, he'll still have the freelancer subconsciously branded as a rank amateur instead of the professional he would like to give the appearance of being.

What are the "Five Cardinal Rules of Manuscript Preparation?" Just these:

To be acceptable, a freelance submission must be:

1. Typewritten, using a pica or elite machine.
2. Double-spaced.
3. In dark black ink only.
4. Generous with margins.
5. On a good grade of white paper, 8½" x 11".

There are absolutely no exceptions to the above rules, with the single possible deviation of permitting use of manuscript paper for No. 5 when requested by an editor. I can think of no other situations which would ever warrant departing from these rules.

Let's examine each one more closely.

• First of all, there is probably not one editor in 100 who will pause long enough to give your work a second glance if it arrives on his desk in longhand, even if you print it meticulously! If you aren't a good typist you really have no business trying to be a writer. You can always employ someone to do your typing for you for a fee, of course, but think how much money you'll lose in the process. I implore you, one more time, if you still hunt-and-peck at the keyboard, sign up for an adult typing class. You *can* become proficient in this skill which is essential to a writer's sustained productivity at little cost and effort.

Also, forget it if you think you'll persuade an editor with fancy typing characters, such as submitting your manuscript in italics, all caps, Old English, script, or other unusual letter styles which are easily adapted to some typewriters by merely changing an element. You'll be noticed by an editor if you use such unusual type faces, all right, but it won't be the kind of notice you desire. Stick to the standard pica or elite typerwriter characters so your manuscripts won't stick out like sore thumbs.

A final word of caution on this subject: If you switch typewriters before completing the typing of a manuscript, be sure your type face is consistent. If you begin with pica, stay with pica. It will make the finished job look better, and will help the editor as he tries to determine how much space will be required for the material you have furnished.

• Secondly, *never* single space a manuscript — the editor needs room to pencil in notations, questions, changes, and corrections — and triple spacing offers more room than is required. A standard form requested by most editors is twenty-five double-spaced lines on a page. This helps him rather quickly calculate how much copy you've submitted, and to know how much space will be required in his publication should he want to use your submission. Again, for conformity's sake, follow the editor's preferences.

• Thirdly, editors are funny people — they don't appreciate manuscripts typed in blue, green, red, or any combination of fancy colors. They like black *only*! (Perhaps it's because black type is easier to read?) Don't show your stripes by typing part or all of your manuscript in a color other than black. If you do, color your work invisible for it may never get from the girl who opens the mail to the editor's desk (on his instructions).

While we're on the subject of ribbons, make sure yours is a dark one, too. When the characters on your paper begin to fade, and/or holes start to appear in the ribbon itself, it's time to replace it.

Keep the keys clean, too. Especially watch for the following letters which may become inked in, particularly with new ribbons: *q, e, o, p, a, d, g, c, b.* Keep a small stiff brush handy and clean the keys as often as necessary. Your editor will sincerely appreciate it.

• Fourthly, the general rule preferred by most editors is that copy stop at least 1¼ inches from all sides of every full page of typewritten manuscript. Again, the reason for this is so the editor will have plenty of room to pencil in notes in the margins.

On the first page of copy, the generally accepted rule is to begin copy about a third of the way down from the top. Certain information is required at the top of this page and on subsequent pages which will be detailed later.

Indentions for paragraphs are generally five spaces, unless you have been advised differently by an editor. Some publications, for instance, only indent two spaces. Some do not indent the initial paragraph.

Of course, if you use manuscript paper, the rules for margins given here will not apply, for in all likelihood you will be advised how many characters an editor wants on a given line, how many spaces he prefers for indentions, and you will probably begin your copy on the top line of the first page, rather than dropping down a third of the way.

A cover page is never a good idea for a freelance article submission, and neither are fancy borders using asterisks and other typewriter or art symbols.

• Fifthly, buff colored paper, off-whites, pastels, and very bright colored stocks are completely out of vogue for editorial submissions. You'll turn an editor off this way about as quickly as any you can name.

Editors don't want odd sizes, either — not even legal size pages, 8½" x' 14". Use white stock, without rules, 8½" x 11" *only*. No exceptions.

There's a wide choice of white stock available, of course, but you'll come out ahead if you stick with a middle-of-the-road sheet. I would suggest about a 20-pound bond with at least 25% cotton fiber content. Your work will look good, feel good, and you can erase mistakes fairly easily on it.

Of course, there are more expensive papers available — slick, 100% rag content papers which really give a plush appearance, but they'll cost considerably more and a lower grade will suffice just as well.

There is also the possibility of buying an inferior grade of paper, too, such as one with all wood content. While this is inexpensive, it is also easily torn, highly absorbent, and causes type to blur as a result of its fuzzy texture. Stay away from this.

These are the five essentials in getting your story from rough draft to finished craft. It is a cardinal sin to break them. If you really want to become a pro, even as a part time hobby, don't violate even one of the five.

But wait! There are some other rules you ought to know and practice, too. While they are secondary in nature, they'll also help you make a good impression on someone on the editorial staff.

We'll group these additional suggestions under seven subdivisions, and examine each one separately: General Rules, Page Form, Sources and Permissions, Carbons, Preparation for Mailing, Copyrighting Your Work, and Cover Letters.

General Rules

1. Strikeovers (typing over the same letter twice) are not permitted in typewritten copy, ever! Take the trouble to clean up your messes!

2. No ink smudges on the paper! Same suggestion about your messes.

3. Clean, neat erasures permissible, or use of white liquid correction fluid. Let it dry thoroughly before you type over it if you use it.

4. Never use staples in a manuscript to hold pages together; never bend or tear corners to connect pages. Rather, use paper clips to bind pages for everything except book-length manuscripts, when no binding is preferable. An empty typewriter paper box will provide a good method of keeping your book manuscript together.

Page Form

Different editors have different preferences here, but if you aren't sure what your editor wants, this form will probably be acceptable:

On the first page of your manuscript, in the upper left-hand corner, single space on four lines your name, street address, city and state and zip code, and your Social Security number. This last bit of information will be helpful to the editor should he desire to purchase your manuscript. By law he is required to record this for later reporting to the IRS. If he is interested in your work, it will save him a letter of request for your number and a response from you if you have already supplied it. Do not view this as being presumptuous on your part, either.

Place nothing in the upper right-hand corner of the first page. Unless I know an editor desires it, I do not state anywhere on the manuscript how many words I have written. To me, doing this does sound a bit presumptuous, for I am telling the editor two things: how many words I've written, and (if he's paying me by the word) not so discreetly, "I'm expecting your count to at least come up to mine." It's not worth haggling over for the few words you may not get paid for.

Besides, if I follow the established pattern of twenty-five double-spaced lines to a page, and tell the editor (in a cover letter) I've supplied copy at 66 characters, for example, he may quickly calculate the approximate number of words I am submitting. Most publishers allow about six characters (including letters, spaces, and punctuation marks) per word.

We've already said you should come down about a third of the way before beginning your article on the first page. Center the title, preferably in all caps.

There are two schools of thought on bylines — one to include, the other to omit. My preference is to omit it because you've already identified yourself at the top of the page. If you choose to include it, however, type "By" and your name centered on the next line under the article's title.

Skip a double-spaced line or two after that before beginning your story.

At the bottom of the first page, type the word "more" without quotation marks but in parentheses. Center it on your page to indicate there are additional pages of copy, in case they get separated from this page. Here is how it should look:

(more)

You will add this to the bottom of each typewritten page except the last one, when you will center the telegrapher's code for 'the end' at the completion of your story, like this:

—30—

At the top of page two, in the upper left-hand corner, type the following on three single-spaced lines: article title, your name, Page 2. Double space a time or two and type twenty-five double-spaced lines of body copy on the page. Incidentally, you will not have gotten twenty-five lines on page one because you started a third of the way down.

Follow the same format on subsequent pages.

Sources and Permissions

Editors are sticklers for knowing precisely where you found the factual data you include in a manuscript. You can be sure an editorial assistant will check such references carefully to be certain you have done your homework properly. If you haven't, and the editor intends to publish your work, you'll get a letter of inquiry into your sources.

The best plan is to type into the right-hand margin of your copy paper where you found reference material, on approximately the same lines on which that material appears in your manuscript. Give the name of the publication, year published, publisher, name of article (if any), author's name, and page numbers where you found the information. Be as complete as you can in providing this information — there's nothing to be gained by omitting some of it.

Permission to use copyrighted material is usually secured by the writer and furnished with the manuscript. Be sure to keep a photostat or carbon of the permission for yourself. Type the exact copyright permission in the right-hand margin also adjacent to the lines it refers to.

Carbons

While not required for manuscript typing, carbons surely are economical and valuable insurance protection!

Most editors don't require carbons but some do, especially if you are writing for them on assignment, and particularly when you are doing lesson course writing. They will usually tell you in advance if a carbon is expected.

For your own peace of mind, however, and to allow you to check anything later you may have a question about, you need one carbon for your own files. Stuff gets lost in the mail every day; why take a chance?

What if you are sure when you see your work in print you never said it that way originally, and you or someone else is embarrassed by it? Without a carbon, you have no proof you didn't say it just that way. For many reasons, carbons are practical ideas.

I prefer packages of carbon sets which may be purchased at stationery stores as opposed to fooling with separate carbon sheets and paper. In the carbon sets the carbon sheet is glued at one end to a thin second sheet (available in white or colors). After typing a page, the carbon may be easily peeled from the face of the second sheet. It's probably a little more expensive than buying paper and carbon sheets separately, but it is quicker, easier, and less messy to use.

If I were buying carbon and second sheets separately, I would choose onionskin paper for the second sheets. This is much easier to make impressions through, resulting in easier-to-read copies. It also requires less space in envelopes when mailing and less space in folders when filing.

Preparation for Mailing

1. *Flat vs. folded.* The generally accepted rule is, if a manuscript is fewer than six pages in length, it may be folded into thirds and inserted into a #10 envelope. If it's six pages or more, submit it flat (without folds) in an envelope at least 9" x 12" or 10" x 13" in dimension.

As noted already, use a stationery box (or one similar in size) to mail book-length manuscripts. You may wish to reinforce corners of your box to avoid crushing. Wrap the box in brown wrapping paper and secure it tightly. You may want to attach a mailing label to it.

2. *Illustrations.* Be sure your name and address are stamped or lightly written on reverse sides of pictures, art work, and other graphics which may accompany your articles. Cutlines should be typed out and taped to picture backs, too. Package pictures facing a stiff piece of cardboard so the post office will not harm them when they are stamped. Mail flat together with your manuscript. Print on the outside of the envelope: PHOTOS — DO NOT FOLD OR BEND.

Incidentally, you will want to use a good quality mailing envelope, one that Uncle Sam will have some difficulty destroying with his battalion of postal machines. A flimsy mailing package may ruin the looks of your material before an editor ever gets a chance to consider it.

3. *Enclose SASE.* Know what that is? Self Addressed Stamped Envelope. Unless you're working on an assignment from an editor, include an envelope bearing sufficient postage for your manuscript to be returned to you. It's just possible the editor won't return unsolicited work if he doesn't want it and you didn't think enough to supply a SASE.

4. *Postage.* Weigh your manuscript in its envelope (and anything else that's going in with it) carefully. Observe mailing zones, and put sufficient postage on your work. This could be a strike against your manuscript if it arrives "Postage Due," particularly if the publisher operates on a shoe-string budget anyway. Don't invite unnecessary irritations.

5. *Insuring your work.* While available, insurance covers the tangible value of what is in the package only, such as paper and illustrations. It does not cover your time, for example. To prevent total loss, keep a carbon.

6. *Which class mail?* My preference is to send manuscripts First Class, although "Special Fourth Class Rate: Manuscript" may be used. First Class costs more and assures faster delivery. Such undeliverable mail is automatically returned to the sender. If you prefer Fourth Class, however, better state on your envelope "Return Postage Guaranteed" under your return address.

You may enclose a personal letter with your work sent under Fourth Class, but you must add enough First Class postage to cover the letter and mark "First Class Letter Enclosed" on the outside of the envelope.

Copyrighting Your Work

It seems to me, especially in the writers' conferences I've attended, there are a lot of freelancers who are hung up on the matter of copyrighting their article submissions. Why? Is copyrighting necessary?

In my opinion, most of the time the answer is "no." The publisher who buys your material usually copyrights it. If you want to have access to it again, for use in some other place in print, all you have to do is write the publisher for permission to do so, giving him full credit as the copyright owner.

There is one exception when I believe a writer should consider copyrighting his material. That is, when one's work is scheduled to appear in a publication which is not copyrighted. You may request the editor to include your own copyright notice, i.e., © 1981 by James H. Cox, with the article as it appears in print.

You may request a "Contribution to a Periodical" form from the Copyright Office. Complete it and return it with $10.00 and two copies of the published work showing your copyright notice. Under the most recent copyright laws, works created after January 1, 1978 may be copyrighted for the life of the author, plus fifty years.

The Copyright Office, Library of Congress, Washington DC 20559 can probably answer any questions you may have about current copyright laws. It offers a number of helpful pamphlets on many varied subjects in this area.

Cover Letters

Once again, there are two schools of thought.

One expert suggests never including a personal letter with a manuscript "unless you have something pertinent to say." His theory is, if the manuscript won't stand on its own without accompaniment, nothing you can say in a letter will alter the situation.

In a sense, he's right. It had better be quality work or you don't stand a chance anyway. But, as an old public relations practitioner, I also believe the cover letter, carefully conceived and thoughtfully composed, can create an atmosphere of acceptance, expectancy, and persuasiveness where none previously existed.

A cover letter, for instance, can tell an editor how the writer was originally attracted to a story, or provide him with additional background surrounding the story which sets the stage for a reading of the manuscript. A writer may establish why he is particularly qualified to write on a given subject. He may use this forum to advise the editor of his interest in having some assignments or of his particular fascination with certain subjects which are frequently treated in the editor's periodical. He may use the cover letter to project a specific idea for one or more future articles.

Is this good PR? You bet. This soft-sell approach has probably done as much for me in gaining present as well as future sales as anything I've ever done.

Let me share with you some excerpts from several letters I've accompanied manuscripts with, all of which sold the first time out.

To the editor of a magazine for church elders:

> Here's a story with a little different twist. A layman is grateful for the man who *used to be* his pastor. The story is real and meaningful to me for I lived it. If you like it, perhaps your readers will like it, too.
>
> The enclosed manuscript was typed at 33 characters, and comes to 129 lines. You could trim some of that if you wish without destroying the content, I imagine.
>
> Keep me in mind for future story ideas. I'll be only too happy to try. Thanks for the consideration you give me.
>
> Cordially yours,
>
> James H. Cox

To the editor of an elementary leaders' magazine:

> I'm appalled at how many churches fail to understand the concept of large group and what it can do for a children's department. I would venture there are several thousand such churches who either do not use it or who see it as a mini worship service tacked on to the 'preliminaries' of the morning. In numerous churches across my own state, the large group is omitted because the church prefers to have the children continue to go to the churchwide opening assembly — or a department opening assembly is still practiced.
>
> Unreal, you say? But it does still exist in many places, and I could cite places if you want to know some. At any rate, I feel so strongly about the value of the large group when utilized as an integral part

of the morning's experiences, I've written a short piece enclosed, "Reinforcement: Large Group's Key Word."

Please look it over and let me know if it has possibilities for your magazine. Thanks for every opportunity of consideration you have given me. There are some things I feel I just must say!

Cordially yours,

James H. Cox

To the editor of a denominational leadership magazine:

I'm enclosing a little article which I think ties in with your audience well, and would appreciate your looking it over for possible use.

You continue to do a splendid job with the magazine and it's one of the few monthlies I truly look forward to coming across my desk.

Best personal wishes for good holidays ahead.

Cordially yours,

James H. Cox

Subtle? Not too, but it helped get each of these articles placed.

You may feel, at least starting out, you don't know an editor well enough to write to him that intimately. But you could sell yourself by writing three or four interesting graphs about you, your background and writing pursuits, and what you'd like to write for him in the future. Don't lay it on too thick, but just a hint of icing never hurt a piece of cake. Try it and see!

Don't Race the Motor 'Til the Light Turns Green

A final thing before leaving the subject of copy preparation. This really has nothing to do with getting your manuscript ready and into the hands of a prospective editor, but rather, what comes next. Do you sit idly by and wait for word from the editor? And how long do you wait?

Let's begin with the second question first. Many religious publishers now acknowledge receipt of unsolicited manuscripts with a preprinted postal card, letting a writer know he will be hearing from them further when an evaluation is completed. However, should you fail to receive such a card, don't come all unglued, for not all publishers go to this additional trouble.

As to how long you should wait, a maximum of two months is generally sufficient for a magazine submission. Some periodicals are often able to report to writers in a much shorter time span. Book manuscripts, on the other hand, almost always take longer, with about three months considered a reasonable waiting period.

Do not bother an editor with inquiries about your work in less time. He has too much else to do. However, if — after two months — you've heard nothing concerning your magazine submission, drop the editor a friendly note asking if your piece is still under consideration. It's possible it may have gotten buried under the stacks on somebody's desk!

Meanwhile, what are you doing in the interim? Hopefully, not resting on your laurels!

This is the time to produce more and more manuscripts. You've done all you can with that one, at least until an editor renders a verdict, so move along to other writing pursuits.

Ideally, you ought to have several manuscripts in the works at all times. The only way to become successful at anything is through practice, and unless you practice the craft you know best, you'll never achieve the potential within you.

Ah, Yes, I Remember It Well

Suppose we review now, to see how much you've learned about moving your story idea from rough draft to finished craft.

Here's a little quiz to help you recall what you've learned. Without looking back over the chapter, or ahead at the answers, see if you can remember these important points. You may wish to write in the book, or answer the questions on a separate sheet of paper.

A. In your own words, give five rules a typist must not violate when preparing a manuscript for publication.

1. ______________________________

2. ______________________________

3. ______________________________

4. ______________________________

5. ____

B. Answer the following with a *T* for *True* statements or *F* for *False* statements in the blanks provided.

1. ______ A standard form requested by most editors is thirty-five double-spaced lines per page.

2. ______ Editors prefer margins of at least 1¼ inches on all sides of copy.

3. ______ Copy should begin a third of the way down on the first page of manuscript paper.

4. ______ A cover page is a good idea for freelance submissions.

5. ______ A 100% rag content paper is recommended.

6. ______ Erasures are permitted on a page.

7. ______ Paper clips are permitted but staples are not.

8. ______ Including a writer's Social Security number on a manuscript may be helpful to an editor.

9. ______ Counting the number of words and typing it on the manuscript is not seen as being presumptuous on a writer's part.

10. ______ The author believes bylines as such are unimportant to a manuscript.

11. ______ If your manuscript is more than six pages in length, it should be mailed flat.

12. ______ Cutlines should be attached to picture fronts.

13. ______ The author believes the cover letter is of little consequence in marketing a manuscript.

14. ______ A magazine article writer ought to hear from an editor about his submission within a month.

15. _____ The writer should move ahead with other writing projects while awaiting an editor's evaluation of a manuscript.

C. Identify.

1. Onionskin: ______________________________
2. SASE: ______________________________
3. Special Fourth Class Rate: ____________________

   ____
4. q,e,o,p,a,d,g,c,b: ________________________
5. Strikeover: ______________________________

Answers (Please don't peek before you try the quiz!)

A. Type it, using a pica or elite machine; double space it; use a dark black ribbon only; leave generous margins; use white paper, 8½" x 11" only.

B. 1. F (25 lines); 2. T; 3. F (begin on top line of manuscript paper but a third of the way down on other paper); 4. F; 5. F (25% will do); 6. T; 7. T; 8. T; 9. F; 10. T; 11. F (after five pages, mail flat); 12. F (to their backs); 13. F; 14. F (two months); 15. T.

C.

1. A thin paper especially good for use with carbons
2. Self Addressed Stamped Envelope
3. Cheaper and slower than First Class; undeliverable mail is not automatically returned to sender
4. Letters which new typewriter ribbons often fill in with ink
5. Typing one letter over another, never a good idea for manuscript submissions

Scoring: Count seven points for each correct answer in A; three points for each correct answer in B; and four points for each correct answer in C. Total your points. A perfect score is 100.

If your score is under 80, you'd better keep this chapter open as a frequent reference when you do the final typing on your freelance submissions for awhile. After all, you don't want to trip yourself up while attempting to put your best foot forward!

7
A Dress Rehearsal for a Nervous Breakdown

All work and no play makes hacks dull boys

Does a rose by any other name smell just as sweet?

Depending on your own church-going experience, you may call *lesson courses* by another name. You may refer to them as "graded series," "graded studies," "uniform series," "curriculum," "basic studies," "quarterlies," or any of a number of other terms. They will be referred to here most often as "lesson courses" or "curriculum pieces," however.

This is the age graded material supplied by a church or denomination for its members to use in studying the Bible and in carrying out other teaching and training experiences. Every evangelical denomination mass produces such literature for study and indoctrination by its members, and a great deal of background preparation goes into this production.

As far as the author knows, all such religious materials are produced for every church *by assignment only*, not merely by freelancers who wish to send in a group of "lessons" to an editor on their own. A freelancer may request an assignment, but until he receives it, he cannot be considered a bonafide writer of curriculum materials.

Herein is the major distinction between all the magazines and publications we have considered up to this point, and lesson course materials. When you write for this latter group, you: (a) have been invited to do so by an editor; (b) know the exact specifications (number of characters, lines, pages) you are to produce; and (c) are almost assured your work will be published.

You could goof up, of course, and fail to see your material in print, but my guess is this happens rather infrequently. An editor has so much invested in a writer in training, preparation, and overhead expense, he checks out a prospect pretty thoroughly before an assignment is offered.

Can he write well? Is he theologically sound? Does he comply with deadlines? These are important questions. If the editor has reason to doubt a prospective writer on any point, he may pass in favor of another candidate.

Demonstrated writing ability often comes as a result of a writer's published manuscripts in freelance periodicals. If one really wants to write curriculum, one of the best routes for getting there is to gain confidence, experience, and to showcase his talents in this manner. In a letter of inquiry to an editor about a curriculum assignment, a writer could refer the editor to some recently published material bearing his by-line, or enclose clippings.

The theological requirement is greater in some circles than in others. Some churches, for instance, require their curriculum writers to be active, practicing members of that church, possibly even working with the specific age group for which they intend to write. Other denominations are less demanding, requiring only that material be produced from a conservative, evangelical stance by a born-again Christian irregardless of faith.

The author is well acquainted, for instance, with a writer who for years has produced reams of curriculum materials for a well known evangelical denomination other than her own. On the other hand, this lady's own church is less open-minded at this point, requiring every writer of its curriculum materials to be a member in good standing of a cooperating local congregation.

An editor wants to be sure his writers will be obedient to their deadlines, also. This is usually spelled out early in his negotiations with a prospective writer, and should be clearly understood by anyone who wishes to write curriculum.

Ah, therein often lies the rub!

A Moonlight Writer's Nightmare

The saddest writing experience of my life was once in doing curriculum. The deadline precipitated that awful experience, but there was more to it than that.

It started out innocently enough. One of my closest buddies, a curriculum editor, asked me to accept a major assignment for his publication. When he verbally assured me I would have thirteen months before the copy was due, I agreed, giving the whole thing little additional thought.

But the nightmare erupted only a couple of months later when I attended a five-day writers' conference to learn what I was expected to produce. I hadn't been there but a few hours before it dawned on me the thirteen months we had first discussed had dissolved, and I was expected to complete the assignment within five months.

My travel itinerary was already set. I was to be away three of those months. I also had to prepare for a three-week summer teaching assignment in the remaining two months, and was just launching a do-it-yourself building project to convert our garage into a study. Obviously, there was no way I could write the first word before the deadline arrived. As the end of the writers' conference approached, I vowed to bow out as gracefully as I could.

But my good editor friend wouldn't take "no" for an answer. He assured me he would "work with me," whatever that meant. I don't think he really realized I meant what I said about there being no time in my schedule to write for at least five months.

Two months later, the week before beginning my travel season, I gave the editor a call. I confessed, in case he hadn't heard me before, I had not written a word. I offered to meet with any other writer of his choice to share everything I had learned at the writers' conference.

My friend would not be thwarted, however. He told me to hang in there, and said he would be "back in touch."

In an hour, he was on the line again.

"How'd you like to have an extra three months?" he pondered.

"An extra three months?" I exclaimed. "Where'd you find them?"

"Oh, sometimes we build extra time into the schedule," he chortled. "I got approval to extend your deadline three months. Can you meet it?"

What could I say?

It was exactly three months later when I got down to the serious business of writing. The travels were behind me for another season, and the converted garage was completed. For the first time I had a writer's hideaway where I could go to compose at my typewriter out of the steady stream of traffic.

In order to finish by the new deadline, I knew I had to make every discretionary hour count. So I devised a plan — agreed to by my supportive wife — that I would enter the private study chamber (which I sometimes thought resembled a gas chamber) Monday through Friday at 5 p.m. and remain locked therein until 11 or

11:30. On Saturdays, I would go in at 8 a.m. and, with the exception of thirty minutes for lunch (time off for good behavior?), I'd remain until 5 or 6 p.m. On Sundays, I started writing after lunch and wrote for several more hours.

Then almost came my undoing. As if that pressure cooker weren't enough, the thing I hadn't figured on was my then two-year-old son, who immediately began to beg, claw, and whine outside the study door, asking over and over again when I could come out. The pull on my heartstrings was almost too much. I probably came about as close to insanity at that point as at any time in my life. In fact, the more my son cried, the more I wanted to spend time with him, and the more I muttered under my breath I would never, ever get myself into that situation again. If there ever was a dress rehearsal for a nervous breakdown, I figured this must surely be it.

At last I turned in the final word of that assignment, having done 400 hours of research, composition, rewrite, and final typing. Now, more than a decade later, I can still say I've kept my vow never to let it happen again. Out of that experience I learned a lot about human endurance and personal sacrifice. This has helped me keep subsequent assignments in their proper perspective, not biting off more than I can chew.

I hope sharing this hasn't been a turn-off to you if you have your heart set on writing curriculum. I've had several lesson course assignments since that one, and currently have one as this book is being written. Yet, I've had the good sense to turn down three or four such assignments when I knew the schedule was already too crowded.

A Humble Origin

I'm deeply appreciative to an editor who decided to take a chance on me early in the decade of the sixties, inviting me to attend a writers' conference with some of the old 'pros' who had been doing curriculum for years. They were such old 'pros,' incidentally, they wrote the material I had studied as a child fifteen years before that! I was duly impressed being in their midst, and I suppose if the President of the United States had been among them I could hardly have been more in awe.

That small beginning led to subsequent writers' conferences in which the editors spelled out precisely what they wanted and how they wanted it and by when. I developed friendships with curriculum writers from all over the nation, and looked forward to future conferences when many of these same writers would gather together for a week. The real discipline of it all would come after that week as we returned home to begin the laborious process of putting our discoveries on paper.

Expenses for the conferences, incidentally, are normally borne by the publication for whom one is writing, from the time you leave home until you return. The conferences are usually closed to anyone who has not been enlisted by an editor to write. Conferences are not necessarily held in an editor's cold, drab, windowless office, either. Often they meet at some state park, or assembly grounds, or even an exotic resort spot. After all, all work and no play makes hacks awfully dull boys.

At the writers' conferences I've attended, participants were given extensive notebooks — each of my binders is 1½ inches thick — with everything a writer needs to know as background for doing his assignment.

Some churches do all of this differently, of course. I am drawing heavily upon mine because I have been there. Some denominations enlist writers by mail and handle everything without a writers' conference. Others have a one-on-one meeting between the editor and individual writers.

Is It True What They Say about Curriculum?

Some time ago I interviewed eleven editors of lesson course periodicals in an attempt to gain some ideas which could be shared with those aspiring to write them. The editors were allowed to give more than one answer to a question. I'll state the questions here, and tell you how many editors gave each answer.

1. How Are Curriculum Writers Selected?

Seven of the eleven replied, "Through an intermediary." This is someone who calls attention to a writer on his own initiative, or recommends him at the writer's request. Having a backlog of published freelance submissions (especially in the church market) is quite helpful for such situations.

Five of the editors answered, "Inquiry to the editor," suggesting the writer took all the initiative to let his availability be known.

Four said their writers come from "writing a sample lesson" which some editors provide potential writers on request. There may or may not be a token payment for such sample lessons. Sometimes an evaluation of the writers' work follows. You may inquire about the availability of sample lessons from any editor you're interested in writing for.

Two said they discovered writers who "submitted a sample of their writing." Again, another case for getting something in print before attempting curriculum.

Only one said curriculum writers are selected by editors who "know the editor personally." Obviously, in this case, it's more important *what* you know rather than *who* you know.

2. *How much is already established for a curriculum writer when his assignment is given him?*

This varies, of course, from periodical to periodical and from church to church. But most of those in this survey mentioned things like lesson titles, texts, number of lines to write, central truths, lesson aims, purposes, and scripture references. It is up to the writer to flesh in the outline, so to speak, with Bible background material and teaching procedures and activities.

3. *About how long does a writer have to complete his assignment?*

The shortest time given was three months and the longest was eighteen months, with all others falling somewhere in between. The average seems to be about six months, however.

If a writer can do so it is best, in my opinion, if he gets a firm deadline in writing from the editor early in their negotiations. This will help him in his schedule planning, as well as reassure him there won't be any last-minute surprises to disrupt his carefully laid plans.

4. *How flexible are deadlines?*

Five of the eleven editors replied, "Not at all." Three said, "A few days." The others replied, "A few weeks."

My best advice is, if you are given a deadline, consider it sacred. Make plans to get your material ready well before it, for a last-minute emergency might wreak havoc on you. Once you are branded for being late your services may not be in great demand again.

5. *How far in advance of publication date is the average assignment given the writer?*

One said four to six months. Five said about two years. The others, three or more years.

This means a writer must often project what will have happened in the intervening time, or what is going to happen several years hence. It takes some guesswork, and when you guess wrong, a member of the editorial staff will probably modify what you have said, if there's time to make changes.

6. *What happens if a writer misses the mark completely? Does he do it over, or does someone else pick it up?*

Seven of the eleven editors said, "If time allows, the writer does the assignment over." Three preferred to use the editorial staff. The remaining one called in another writer from the outside to pick up the pieces and put them in acceptable order.

I've known editors who had to pick up the ball and run with it themselves when writers backed out half way through an assignment, or when a writers' work was so poorly prepared it was not usable. I guess that's why I never wanted to be an editor, for I've seen those grief-stricken stares in their eyes. The editors usually aren't paid for their overtime work, either.

Of course, the writer is almost always permanently disbarred from future consideration on those publications, and this may affect his or her potential sales to other editors as well. It's a no-win situation for everybody involved.

7. *Briefly, what suggestions would you give the aspiring writer for your publication?*

I'm going to compile the editors' answers here, listing without comment the suggestions they gave, all of which are good:

- Write clearly, spell well
- Do not write above the age level
- Use illustrations to make a point
- Clear your calendar for writing
- Avoid too much activity during the time of writing
- How can I know you're there unless I hear from you?

Do you still want to write curriculum? I think you will find it challenging, stimulating, and time-consuming if you do. But there will be rewards, too. You'll do a lot of growing mentally, emotionally, and spiritually. And, you will be able to point with pride to this new pinnacle of achievement you've reached.

If you really don't have that interest, and particularly if you don't have time to devote to it, and you can't withstand the rigors of meeting the deadlines, my advice is to pass this one up. Curriculum writing simply isn't for everybody.

Once, when I was under a lot of pressure, I considered accepting another curriculum assignment. But a wise editor friend (on yet another publication) gave me some very timely advice: "Certainly you won't do it for the money," he implored, "and the notoriety is nothing for you've seen your byline in print before." That made sense to me. I phoned the editor and turned down the assignment.

Look before you leap! But, if you feel you can handle it, don't hesitate. It just may be your crowning achievement as a religious freelancer.

8
You'll Never Get Rich

Satisfaction could be its own reward

We have almost completely avoided the subject of rates paid to freelance writers for their submissions to the church market. I didn't want to disillusion anyone before he finished reading the book! (In case you haven't figured it out yet, I've saved some rather disconcerting news for the end.)

Reader's Digest is offering writers several thousand dollars on acceptance for its First Person and Premonition article series as this book goes to print. It further pays $300 for "Life in These United States," dropping down to $35 for "Laughter, the Best Medicine," "Personal Glimpses," and "Quotable Quotes."

Sports Illustrated, on the other hand, currently provides writers' fees of $300 for regional pieces to $1,250 and up for longer texts.

Women's magazines predominate in the consumer market.

McCall's Magazine states its rates for most articles and stories are negotiable, though some are set, such as $1,000 for "Women on the Job."

Another women's magazine, *Redbook*, reports its typical writers' payments include $500 for contributions to "Young Mother's Story," $850 for short short fiction, and $1,000 and up for regular length stories. "Article rates depend on length, subject, and amount of research," said an editor. "The Redbook Novel" starts at $7,500.

Of course, this is only a sample of the national slicks to give you an idea of what freelancers are now being paid.

Why am I telling you all this? Not because I'm a good guy for you're going to learn rather quickly (and painfully) religious publishers for the most part don't begin to touch these payment levels. All of this somehow reminds me of the fellow I once worked with who was given a ten percent raise, and who then remarked to his peers, "Ten percent of nothing is still nothing." It's really not that bad, but it's close.

A Logical Explanation, or Maybe Two, or Three

Of course, what one must keep in perspective is these comparatively high rates paid to writers by the national consumer magazines are partially drawn from (1) expensive subscriptions with (2) very large circulations. Those magazines may generate (3) hundreds of thousands of dollars of advertising revenue in a single issue, too.

I was appalled a couple of years ago when one of my favorite national magazines offered me a 'bargain' one-year subscription plan of $39.00 for fifty-two issues. While that's only seventy-five cents a week, that was still about twice what my pocketbook could afford. There are plenty of people who can and do spend $39.00 and more for a year's worth of magazines, however.

Church publications, on the other hand, may be sold on a cost recovery or break-even basis. Even when a profit is involved, that margin is often purposely kept low so as many persons as possible may have access to the literature.

In the case of curriculum materials, it is almost essential that every church have literature pieces for each of its active members. If a large profit was anticipated, the church literature would be prohibitive for some smaller parishes and congregations to purchase.

Circulation of the magazines also plays a part in determining what writers are paid.

In a recent year *Reader's Digest* guaranteed its advertisers it had a circulation of almost eighteen million subscribers! (What magazine among religious periodicals can come anywhere close?) *Sports Illustrated* claimed 2.4 million that year; *McCall's*, 6.25 million; and *Redbook*, 4.3 million.

The truth is, few religious periodicals ever reach that many people. Currently, only one is believed to top a million — *Decision*, published by the Billy Graham Evangelistic Association. Its monthly circulation reached 2.8 million subscribers as this book went to press.

Also, most religious magazines carry little or no paid advertising, in contrast with the popular consumer periodicals, whose major source of revenue is often ad sales.

These, then, are some of the reasons why religious periodicals can't begin to compete with the national consumer magazines in payments to freelancers. When a writer understands and accepts these realities, he may find working on this reduced scale much more palatable, particularly if he has been accustomed to receiving higher wages from other markets.

Just what do religious publishers pay? I'm relying upon the publishers themselves for information. Rates may have increased slightly since these figures were released at the end of 1980.

I'll not try to name them all, but will give a random sampling of some prominent ones. In order, the listings include the name of the periodical, the city in which it is published, publisher (if separate), circulation, and rate of payment to freelance writers.

Baptist Leader: Valley Forge, PA; American Baptist Churches in the USA; 15,000; $15-$40.

Biblical Illustrator: Nashville, TN; Sunday School Board of the Southern Baptist Convention; 82,000; three-and-a-half cents a word. (Freelance submissions discouraged.)

The Christian Century: Chicago, IL; 30,000; $25-100.

Christian Herald: Chappaqua, NY; 285,000; $300 maximum.

Christianity Today: Carol Stream, IL; 180,000; $100 minimum, $200 maximum.

The Church Herald: Grand Rapids, MI; Reformed Church in America; 72,000; about three cents per word.

Decision: Minneapolis, MN; Billy Graham Evangelistic Association; 2.8 million; $125 minimum, $250 maximum, $10-$40 for poetry.

Light And Life: Winona Lake, IN; Free Methodist Publishing House; 58,000; three cents per word.

The Lutheran: Philadephia, PA; Lutheran Church in America; 594,000; $60 per printed page used in the magazine.

The Lutheran Standard: Minneapolis, MN; American Lutheran Church; 590,000; about five cents per word.

Message Magazine: Nashville, TN; Southern Publishing Association of Seventh-Day Adventists; 100,000; two cents per word.

Moody Monthly: Chicago, IL; 300,000; ten cents per word.

New Era: Salt Lake City, UT; The Church of Jesus Christ of Latter-Day Saints (Mormon); 180,000; three to six cents per word.

Our Sunday Visitor: Huntington, IN; Catholic Church; 340,000; $75 minimum, $200 maximum.

Pentecostal Evangel: Springfield, MO; The General Council of the Assemblies of God; 280,000; about two cents a word.

These Times: Nashville, TN; Southern Publishing Association of Seventh-Day Adventists; 220,000; seven to ten cents per word.

Of course, this list doesn't scratch the surface of religious publications currently available. Yet, it does give some idea of what a freelance writer in the church market may expect to receive in compensation for his words.

Years ago, I fantasized what life would be like if I terminated my 9-to-5 job, forgot about regular paychecks, and wrote to my heart's content. Yet, every time I realized I would be paying my own self employment taxes, providing my own retirement program, underwriting my own medical and hospitalization insurance, and would seldom be able to take a vacation or holiday, I got cold feet.

I knew an editor friend who quit his job in favor of working for himself as a religious freelancer. He once told me, for his family of four, he had to clear $1,000 monthly or go under. (This was years ago, of course.) His wife supported him by doing heavy research, supplying reference material he could draw upon as he composed at the typewriter. He sought, and got, every assignment he possibly could, but it was not enough. After a year of it he went back to edit for the publisher he had left.

Unless you've got a lot of fortitude, and some hefty savings salted away for *many* rainy days, I'd think twice before cutting the strings from a regular paycheck to freelance for church publications. In fact, if I were the sole breadwinner for three or more persons, I would not seriously consider such a risk.

For a different point of view, I suggest you check out the book, *How You Can Make $20,000 a Year Writing* by Nancy Hanson, in the Appendix. I believe this could possibly be feasible if a full time freelancer submitted only nominal amounts of his work to religious publishers, relying on other markets which she suggests as his staples.

Religious Writing: It Doesn't Make Cents

Up to this point, we have dealt exclusively with monetary rewards for freelancing. The title of this chapter is, "You'll Never Get Rich," and if one applies this solely to what he earns as a writer for church periodicals, this is probably true. Yet, here's one writer that's just as convinced there are other considerations which should be given this whole spectrum of freelancing. It seems to me there are a number of intangibles which far outweigh the monetary compensation religious writers receive for their efforts.

Here are some of those rewards:

• *Intensive Bible study.* One of the joys I continue to derive, particularly from my experiences as a curriculum writer, is how much I have learned from concentrated biblical research.

Let me state flatly I am not scholarly. I poured through forty-five different commentaries, Bible handbooks, atlases, and related helps for one assignment on the life of Moses, however. This was soon followed by yet another assignment on Moses' life. By the time I finished all that digging, I considered myself something of an authority on the exodus! I didn't know a whole lot about other portions of scripture, but I sure felt I could identify every shrub on Mt. Sinai!

All of this has been translated into meaningful dialog in teaching experiences on Sunday mornings in my own church. When a writer digs into the Word, he gets a whole lot more for later consumption, too.

• *A deeper devotional life.* Can you study the Word of God, and write of spiritual things, without feeling the presence of the great *I Am*? Doesn't what you write help you harmonize your own life more fully with his?

Sometimes I stop writing and marvel how God loved me so, how he chose me to receive this talent of writing, and how he created such a wonderful world for me to enjoy. I often thank him right then for his goodness and his presence in my life.

Hopefully, the words we write, the research we do, the experiences we have as writers — joys and frustrations alike — will strengthen our commitment as Christians, and lift us to loftier heights.

• *Improved reading ability.* My wife is one of the fastest readers I know. I have always marveled at this, and have been a bit envious, too. While I don't read nearly as rapidly as she does, I am sure my own reading ability has been enhanced because of the billions and billions of words I've encountered while doing research for writing projects, working against strict deadlines much of the time. I simply *had* to learn to read faster. I'm grateful for this side benefit to my writing. Surely others have experienced it, too.

• *Better use of time.* Have you ever despised the hours you foolishly frittered away in front of a TV set, not really enjoying the program but being too lazy to turn it off, or to move on to something productive? I have. I've also wasted a lot of additional time overeating, napping, engaging in prolonged telephone conversations which didn't interest me, mind-wandering on trivial things, and attending non-productive meetings which were perfectly boring.

Aren't human beings silly? We have twenty-four hours a day, yet we say there's "never enough time." We even look for 'busy work' so we will *appear* to be occupied!

When I've got a writing project going, however, all those extra hours I usually waste seem to evaporate. My concentration is on a higher level: there is purpose for the discretionary hours I have. As a result, I feel like a more productive individual. Time is one of the resources God gave me, too. I feel obligated to use it wisely.

- *An opportunity to help others.* I suspect, more than any of us ever realizes, the words we produce as writers influence scores, or hundreds, or even thousands of unknown readers who reflect upon their messages. I have been surprised in traveling over the nation to encounter people who tell me how something I have written months or even years earlier has touched their lives. You may have had the same experience.

When this happens, it's a reminder God is working through me just as he does ministers, although my pulpit is not a podium but a printed page. How powerful and how sacred is this obligation!

Some readers have come to know a saving knowledge of Jesus Christ through what a writer has written. Others have turned their lives around, recommitting themselves to a closer walk with Jesus. When life seemed to hold no meaning, still others found reasons for living in literature. None of us will ever know how much eternal good the words we write produce. But let us not linger over that. If we have the gift, we have the obligation.

You will probably never get rich when you write for the church — if you weigh it solely from a monetary perspective. The real rewards have enduring values, however, and no price tag may ever be placed upon them. When you write for a religious market, you lay up for yourself "treasures ... where neither moth nor rust doth corrupt, and where thieves do not break through and steal " (Matt. 6:20).

A Final Word

Have you now come to a new appreciation of this thrilling opportunity called writing? Perhaps you were not at all sure you had the gift. Perhaps you were too afraid to use it. If I have accomplished any purpose, maybe I have made you at least willing to try.

My favorite comedienne is Minnie Pearl, the gossip of Grinder's Switch, Tennessee. Although I have heard the story many times, I still love it when she tells about leaving Grinder's Switch in 1940 to come to Nashville to appear on the Grand Ole Opry for the first time.

One of the principal 'characters' of Grinder's Switch is an old maid by the name of Lizzie Tinkum. You get the feeling there are lots of old maids at Grinder's Swtich, and all of them are man-crazy, including Minnie, but that's beside the point.

As Minnie leaves home for the big city that day, Lizzie tells her about all the handsome "fellers" she will find up there. She asks Minnie to grab every one of them she sees and give 'em a big hug for her.

Minnie, of course, dutifully tells Lizzie she'll be only too happy to oblige!

With much embellishment, Minnie tells her audience about the first good lookin' "feller" she encounters on a Nashville street. She throws her arms around him and gives him a big hug, "Just for Lizzie, not for me."

The second man she meets, she goes through the same routine again, cautiously advising the audience it's all "Just for Lizzie, not for me."

The third experience is the same, still, "Just for Lizzie, not for me."

"And then," she says, her eyes flashing, her audience in knowing expectancy, her words deliberate: "Then I seen that handsome Roy Acuff. And that's when I decided to go into business for myself!"

She never fails to bring the house down every time!

If God has given you the talent of writing, and you've made the commitment to go into business for yourself (even avocationally), what are you waiting for? The scriptures admonish, "For unto whomsoever much is given, of him shall be much required" (Lk. 12:48).

You'll never get rich. But really, how can you possibly lose?

Appendix

If you are looking for every title currently in book stores and on library shelves to help freelancers break into writing, you will be disappointed in this list. There are too many volumes coming out every year to list them all in the first place. Besides, there is a purpose in listing the volumes we have.

With few exceptions, most deal exclusively with breaking into the church market, as opposed to writing for general consumer magazines and other secular-oriented media. The exceptions deal primarily with better clarity and grammar in writing, something the religious scribe needs just as much as that one writing for a secular audience.

I have included a few comments about each book to help you decide which ones might be of greatest help to you. I have read or thoroughly examined each volume myself before recommending it to be certain it can offer something helpful to writers in this market.

Meanwhile, as you have opportunity, and as your horizons and interests broaden, you will profit from spending several hours in a good book store or library checking out the current titles for those who want to break into any type of freelancing. Some are sure to make you thirst for their contents, and if you're in a book store, in a moment of weakness you may do what I do — reach for your wallet. But if you're serious about what you're doing, and not just intending to write "some day," your investment will probably be well worth it all.

Anderson, Margaret J., *The Christian Writer's Handbook* (New York: Harper & Row, Publishers, 1974). A widely published Christian writer takes her readers step-by-step through the publishing process: from discovering ideas to obtaining rights and privileges, from submitting materials to organizing a filing system. She gives examples and notes pitfalls to be avoided in producing meditations, columns, poetry, interviews, how-to articles, narratives, fiction, short stories, quizzes, and puzzles. 270 pp.

Browne, Benjamin P., editor, *Christian Journalism for Today: A Resource Book for Writers and Editors* (Philadelphia: The Judson Press, 1952); *The Writers' Conference Comes to You* (1956); *Techniques of Christian Writing* (1960). All three volumes are largely collections of lectures from the National Christian Writers and Editors' Conference at Green Lake, Wisconsin, plus other seminars. Lecturers, successful writers themselves, cover such topics as fiction, articles, features, play writing, books, poetry, writing for children, and more. Each volume is inspirational, motivational, and filled with techniques. 252 pp., 424 pp., 382 pp. respectively. Same publisher.

Flesch, Rudolph, *How to Write, Speak, and Think More Effectively* (New York: Harper & Row, Publishers, 1960). Includes triple tests for measuring sentence readability, plus twenty-five rules for effective writing. This is a step-by-step course in writing, speaking, and thinking in a systematic program of mind self-improvement. Exercises, examples, detailed analyses, tests, and summaries included. 362 pp.

Gunning, Robert, *How to Take the Fog Out of Writing* (Chicago: The Dartnell Corp., 1964). An inexpensive, condensed paperback version of Gunning's widely received earlier work, *The Technique of Clear Writing*. The Fog Index is explained, along with ten principles of clear writing, and twenty-five ways of cutting through useless jargon in writing. A good investment for the novice and seasoned writer. 64 pp.

Gunning, Robert, *The Technique of Clear Writing* (New York: McGraw-Hill Book Co., Inc., 1952). The Fog Index, Gunning's famous test for readability, is detailed, based on sentence length and number of multisyllable words used. Included are ten ways to increase readability. All of it, when applied against a freelancer's own work, may be a fascinating — and sometimes, humiliating — experience. 289 pp.

Hanson, Nancy Edmonds, *How You Can Make $20,000 a Year Writing (No matter where you live)* (Cincinnati: Writer's Digest Books, 1980). Disputes nearly everything we said in chapter eight, but this book is for those who definitely plan to go beyond religious freelancing. It's possible, says this writer, to earn in excess of $20,000 annually, to do it with magazine articles, easy access markets, photography, books, ghost writing, audiovisuals, commercial writing, and the like. Surely religious periodicals could contribute to all this. Offers convincing arguments for quitting one's permanent job. 270 pp.

Harral, Stewart, *Patterns of Publicity Copy* (Norman: University of Oklahoma Press, 1950). While written from the standpoint of a publicity copy or news release writer, the principles contained are still good ones for religious freelancers: the lead for your story is vital, the words you choose must transmit emotion to the reader, and story ideas may be located in unusual places. A check list for your manuscript copy is included. 139 pp.

Hastings, Robert J., *How I Write: A Manual for Beginning Writers* (Nashville: Broadman Press, 1973). A successful freelancer in the church market tells how he started, gives a dozen rules to help the would-be writer become successful, and passes on other personal tips to make the "hard work" of writing easier. A religious newspaper editor, Hastings discourages book writing, encourages syndicated column writing, and takes a look at church news writing on the side. 145 pp.

Polking, Kirk; Chimsky, Jean; and Adkins, Rose, editors, *The Beginning Writer's Answer Book* (Cincinnati: Writer's Digest Books, 1978). Contains 567 questions most frequently asked editors of *Writer's Digest* and answered by three professionals in the field of writing. Deals with copyright laws, trends in the marketplace, editorial taboos, manuscript preparation, ways to avoid libel and plagiarism, and tips for increasing sales. Categories arranged for convenience and a comprehensive cross index provided. For secular and religious markets. 270 pp.

Schell, Mildred, *Wanted: Writers for the Christian Market* (Valley Forge: Judson Press, 1975). This book is divided into two sections — one dealing with the writer himself, the other with needs of religious periodicals. It even includes a "mini-grammar." Short fiction, nonfiction, curriculum, and books are highlighted in separate chapters. The author has been a writer and editor of children's Church School materials. 160 pp.

Walker, Robert; Franzen, Janice; and Kidd, Helen, editors, *The Successful Writers and Editors' Guidebook* (Carol Stream: Creation House, 1977). The kind of gift book any freelancer would appreciate for himself. Heavily illustrated, it contains eighty-five short but extremely helpful articles by successful religious editors, writers, and publishers in an extensive collection. More than 300 markets for religious books, articles, photos, short stories, and poetry included. It's delightful reading, the kind you can bite off in small pieces and savor. 506 pp.

Wirt, Sherwood Eliot, *You Can Tell the World: New Directions for Christian Writers* (Minneapolis: Augsburg Publishing House, 1975). How the writer gets ideas, how to organize material, how to write with sparkle, how to submit material to publishers, and how and when to rewrite are emphasized by the editor emeritus of *Decision* magazine. He covers the basic tools and reference books for Christian writing, plus offers motivation, inspiration, and direction for the novice or experienced writer. 127 pp.

Wolseley, Roland E., editor, *Writing for the Religious Market* (New York: Association Press, 1956). Although written by eighteen religious writers a quarter of a century ago, the messages in this book are still timely. Subjects deal with curriculum, devotional books, drama, inspirational and juvenile fiction, magazine articles, newspaper features, news reporting, novels, poetry, publicity, and more. Secular and religious media are considered for each writing form, where applicable. 304 pp.

Writer's Market (Cincinnati: Writer's Digest Books, published annually). The largest, most comprehensive "supermarket for writers" ever assembled, now approaching 5,000 places freelancers can sell short stories, plays, gags, greeting card verse, scripts, fillers, and lots more. The annual volume gives names and addresses of editors, how much they pay, and how a writer may meet their editorial needs. A large section is devoted to religious publications. An extremely valuable tool for any freelancer. 1000 pp. plus.